Unstoppable will encourage you to run the race God has placed before you with new confidence, no matter what the circumstances. It will remind you that God can and will use anyone who trusts him fully and relies on his strength.

JOYCE MEYER, Bible teacher and bestselling author

Christine's passion is impressive from a distance, and even more inspirational up close. Every time I'm around her, I'm reminded of how great an impact one person can make. She believes that God's power is limitless and his purpose is unstoppable. Her faith is contagious, and I believe after reading this book you'll discover the same passion to run your race for God's glory.

STEVEN FURTICK, lead pastor, Elevation Church and *New York Times* bestselling author of *Crash the Chatterbox* and *Greater*

Chances are, most days you don't feel unstoppable. But God has a calling for your life that involves faith, perseverance, and possibly even danger. In Christine Caine's amazing book, *Unstoppable*, she will inspire and instruct you to run your unique race—and with Christ's help, nothing will stop you from glorifying God.

CRAIG GROESCHEL, senior pastor of LifeChurch.tv and author of *Fight: Winning the Battles that Matter Most*

UNSTOPPABLE

UNSTOPPABLE

CHRISTINE CAINE

UNSTOPPABLE

Step into Your Purpose,

Run Your Race,

Embrace the Future

 ZONDERVAN®

ZONDERVAN

Unstoppable
Copyright © 2014, 2018 by Christine Caine

Requests for information should be addressed to:
Zondervan, *3900 Sparks Dr. SE, Grand Rapids, Michigan 49546*

ISBN 978-0-310-35136-8 (softcover)

ISBN 978-0-310-35360-7 (ebook)

Library of Congress Cataloging-in-Publication Data

Caine, Christine.
  Unstoppable : running the race you were born to win / Christine Caine. -- 1st [edition].
    pages cm
    Includes bibliographical references.
    ISBN 978-0-310-34117-8 (softcover)
  1. Christian life. I. Title.
BV4501.3.C3355 2014
248.4--dc23   2014008438

Published in association with the literary agency of David O. Middlebrook, 4501 Merlot Avenue, Grapevine, Texas 76051.

Study Guide written by Christine Anderson
Cover photograph: Nate Griffin | @kanakanate
Interior design: Greg Johnson/Textbook Perfect

First printing March 2018 / Printed in the United States of America

To my pastors, Brian and Bobbie Houston.
Thank you for taking a risk and giving me the opportunity
to step into my lane and run my race.
I love you both dearly.

CONTENTS

CHAPTER 1

THE DIVINE RELAY

I grabbed Nick's hand and, for what must have been the hundredth time, said, "I can't believe we're here at the Olympics! The Olympics, Nick! Isn't it awesome?"

He could barely hear me above the roar of the crowd, but he didn't need to. He could read not only my lips but the glow on my face and could feel the electricity in the air.

"Awesome!" he shouted back, squeezing my hand.

We took in the view together — the massive stadium filled with light and color and motion and 110,000 spectators, the buzz of conversations in who knew how many languages, the red track below surrounding the vibrant green and stunning yellow infield, and the runners taking their positions.

The year was 2000 — Saturday, September 30. The place, Sydney, in my homeland of Australia. I'd celebrated my thirty-fourth birthday a week before, and being here felt like the best birthday gift of my life. I was mesmerized by the sheer size of this state-of-the-art stadium. It made me feel so tiny, a speck in this massive crowd, yet I felt connected, as if being here bonded me to every Olympic athlete and every spectator since the first Olympic Games in ancient Greece.

Though I'm Australian by birth, Greek blood runs through my veins. I am Greek through and through. The image of the five interlocking Olympic rings fluttering on the Olympic flags above us and plastered all over Sydney — in fact, all over the world — made my heart swell and my chin lift at the thought of the ancient Greek tradition that had inspired all these nations to join together in promoting a peaceful and better world through sportsmanship, friendship, solidarity, and fair play. You got it — I was bedazzled, sold out, and on fire with Olympic spirit!

I love all things sport and always have. I competed as a runner in high school, and running is still my favorite workout. As a spectator, I've always been partial to the 4 x 100-meter relay, and the women's relay in particular. It seemed too good to believe that my husband, Nick, and I were about to watch this very race in person. Eight countries were competing in the final race for gold. I was cheering for the USA team to take the medal.

THE LEGACY

Before the 2000 Sydney Olympics, the USA women's 4 x 100-meter relay team had won the gold medal nine times out of sixteen Olympics. Coming into this race, they were the reigning Olympic champions, having won the gold in 1996. As they prepared to carry on that legacy, I was ready to cheer them on to victory.

Nick and I watched the runners moving onto the track, four per team. The energy of the crowd surged as the teams were announced and cameras zoomed in on the runners' faces, magnifying them on the massive screen that seemed to float in the evening sky. White lines marked the three exchange zones, each 20 meters in length, in every lane. The first runner, the starter, would cover about 100 meters and enter the first exchange zone to meet the second runner, who would already be running, arm stretched out behind, hand open, ready to receive the baton that had to be handed off within that 20-meter exchange zone. Runner two would carry the baton to the second exchange zone and hand off the baton to runner three, who in turn would run about 100 meters, handing off the baton to the anchor, who would carry it across the finish. The entire race would be only one lap, 400 meters, and take less than one minute.

The runners took their positions — starters at their staggered starting blocks, the second and third runners and the anchors at their places in their respective exchange zones. The raucous noise of thousands of people suddenly quieted. A hush fell over the crowd. The tension was palpable. I held my breath, awaiting the start gun.

The shot rang out and they were off. The first USA handoff was smooth, and my screaming cheers were lost in the roar around me as the US team took the lead. But in the next exchange zone, the second runner struggled to get the baton into the third runner's hand. My heart fell. That muffed handoff had cost precious milliseconds and perhaps the race, but I hoped the third and fourth runners could make up for it.

The seconds flew by — 41.95 seconds to be exact. That's how long it took for Bahama to win the gold. Jamaica was a mere .18 seconds behind, followed by the USA, at 42.20 seconds, trailing the winning team by .25 seconds.[1]

"Nick, they should have won!" I cried in disbelief. "How did this happen?" He didn't need to answer. I'd seen it with my own eyes. It had happened in the fraction of a second in the second handoff, when precious time was lost. I watched the screen replay the final seconds at the finish line. Exhilaration on the face of the Bahamian anchor, disbelief on the face of the American. I thought my heart would break for her and her team. All the years of practice, the discipline, the single-minded focus that had led up to this moment, and the gold was gone. One sloppy exchange and the USA championship was relinquished.

"At least they medaled," Nick said, trying to comfort me. "They won the bronze."

I scowled back at him. Those women hadn't come for the bronze. They'd come for the gold. They were running to *win*. Now they'd need to wait four years to win back the gold.

~~~~~~

Four years passed.

In a hotel room somewhere in the US, on August 27, Nick and I sat in front of a television, captivated by scenes of the 2004 Summer Olympics in Athens, Greece. My Greek pride swelled at the stunning pageantry of the opening ceremonies, and I drank in the history and imagery of every broadcast. My eyes were glued to the screen every available moment, but never was my anticipation higher than when Team USA — LaTasha Colander, Lauryn Williams, Marion Jones, and Angela Williams — took their places for the first round of the qualifying heats of the women's 4 x 100 relay.

Sixteen teams were competing in the two-heat qualifying round. Eight teams would win their place in the final race. The four American women were considered the four fastest runners on the field. Poor Nick was nearly deaf from my screams of joy when they proved themselves to be the fastest and strongest team in the first heat that day: 41.67 seconds!

"Nick, they were faster than the winning team in 2000. Tomorrow, the gold is theirs for sure, right?"

The next day, nothing could have kept me away from watching the finals, the medal race. The four American women took their positions, muscles swelling, faces alive with focus and concentration. I couldn't wait to watch them win, poetry in motion, precision and power in every move. When Marion Jones, the second runner, received her baton and accelerated, I knew nothing would stop this incredible team. She approached Lauryn Williams for the second exchange of the baton. But my heart dropped.

"No!" I screamed, jumping to my feet. "No way!"

I still don't know exactly what went wrong. Had Lauryn started too early, too fast? Was Marion too far behind? But no matter which of them was at fault, their timing was off. When that baton finally passed from Marion's forward thrusting arm to Lauryn's back-stretched hand, they had run *out* of the exchange zone. The handoff came too late.

I was stunned. But they were the fastest! They were the strongest! They had the lead! They were the best!

It didn't matter. The 20-meter exchange zone is clearly marked. The passing of the baton must take place within that zone or the team is out of the race. Not only did they miss the gold, they were disqualified. Stopped in their tracks. Not even a *bronze* medal. Disbelieving, I watched them stop running and walk off the track. Once again, they were undone in the exchange zone.

"How could this happen?" I cried.

Nick was a wise enough husband not to offer a response. (Lesson learned four years earlier.)

Fast-forward to Beijing in 2008, the semifinals — Thursday, August 21. This year, Nick and I, again traveling in ministry, watched from a cottage in the town of Ulverston, Cumbria, England. Exchange one — perfect! Exchange two — ideal! Whew! I was on my feet, screaming. Leading the race, Torri Edwards reached forward for that final exchange to Lauryn Williams ...

Can you feel the tension? I suspect that Nick had the paramedics on hold this time, just in case.

What happened next is still seared in my memory — the image of that baton slipping from Lauryn Williams's grasp and hitting the track. She dropped the baton! Dropped it! And with it the hopes and dreams of every fan of Team USA. Disqualified in the semifinals! For the first time in forty-eight years,[2] Team USA wouldn't even run in the final medal race. My jaw dropped. I was speechless, which, if you ask Nick, was a miracle in itself.

THE GAMES GO ON AND ON AND ON . . .

I confess. By the time of the London 2012 games, twelve years since I'd witnessed that first disappointing loss, I was afraid to watch the women's 4 x 100 relay.

Not that I was going to let that stop me, of course. I assumed it was my love of the games, my love of the sport that kept drawing me back to watch the games, but God had another reason for instilling within me a passion for the relay race. He had something important he wanted me to see.

This time, I was in America with Nick and our girls. We joined the 219.4 million Americans tuning in to the NBC coverage, making the 2012 Olympic Games the most watched event in US TV history. On Friday, August 10, 2012, eight countries — thirty-two runners — once again took their places. Team USA was in lane 7, and my heart, though pounding in trepidation, was right there with them.

I knew that the USA runners were at the top of their game. Tianna Madison, Allyson Felix, Bianca Knight, and Carmelita Jeter had nailed the qualifying round at the stunning speed of 41.64 seconds.[3] These runners were brilliant! But this time I knew that did not mean victory was secure. I'd witnessed the best of the best, the fastest of the fast, the most powerful, and the favored lose the race three times before. Sydney in 2000. Athens in 2004. Beijing in 2008. Bitter experience had taught me a few things:

- Having the fastest runner doesn't necessarily win the race.
- Having the fastest team doesn't necessarily win the race.

- Having the most experienced or the most dedicated runners doesn't necessarily win the race.
- Having the reigning champions or the contenders determined to reclaim their championship doesn't necessarily win the race.

None of these things will win the race unless the baton is safely passed in each and every exchange zone and carried first across the finish line. If it isn't, the entire team loses.

In a relay, everything hinges on what happens in the exchange zone.

And that's when it hit me — this lesson from God twelve years in the making.

I wasn't just watching an Olympic race. I was seeing a crystal-clear representation of how the church must work and what happens when it doesn't. As those athletes moved into position in London in 2012, I was seeing the church lined up in lanes all over the globe, batons in hand, running the race that matters most in this world — the divine relay!

This divine relay is filled with exchange zones. If the baton of faith passes fluidly from person to person, from generation to generation, we speed unstoppable toward the finish line. But if the exchange is fumbled, the whole team, the whole church, suffers.

By this time in my life, I'd been traveling across the globe for years doing ministry. Nick and I had been serving the local church and leaders through Equip & Empower Ministries and then through The A21 Campaign — an organization we founded in 2008 dedicated to abolishing injustice in the twenty-first century, focused on stopping human trafficking. Through Equip & Empower, as well as The A21 Campaign, I was learning just how important it is to get the "exchange zone" right to ensure that no runners stop running and walk off the field, but that every runner becomes unstoppable in their dedication to carry their baton of faith to the next runner.

I was in one of those lanes myself. I'd been running the race God called me to run. I'd been handed quite a few batons along the way and had released many, some smoothly, some not so well. I had many batons I needed to deliver to the next runners. How could I do it with excellence? What would keep me, or the runners after me, from fumbling or dropping or even stopping the passing of their batons from one to another?

I thought of my A21 team working in dangerous places around the world to fight human trafficking. Was I training them to run well, to receive and hand off so that the whole team could win and the kingdom of God could move forward? I thought of believers I'd met around the world who were running well and others who'd dropped their batons or walked out of the race completely.

The divine relay is tough. The track is treacherous. There are so many ways to mangle the exchange zones, to overshoot, to be knocked off the track, to drop the baton, to stop running. The church needs champion runners who never give up, who persevere no matter what they encounter, who run to win — unstoppable, no matter the cost.

As the camera scanned the passionate crowd that filled the Olympic stadium that day, Hebrews 12:1 – 2 flew into my mind:

> *Therefore, since we are surrounded by such a great cloud of witnesses, let us throw off everything that hinders and the sin that so easily entangles. And let us run with perseverance the race marked out for us, fixing our eyes on Jesus, the pioneer and perfecter of faith.*
>
> HEBREWS 12:1 – 2

The first verse describes a great cloud of witnesses. I considered the millions of people watching the 2012 games all over the globe. Did this compare with "a great cloud of witnesses"?

Not hardly.

Not compared to eternity! Not compared to the countless believers who have come before us and who will come after us. This was but a glimpse, a shadow, of how great God's cloud of witnesses really is. I may be passionate about sports, about running, about the Olympic Games, but my passion for those things pales in comparison with the one thing I am most passionate about — the cause of Jesus Christ. The combined passion of all those Olympic witnesses, the passion for this race, these games, was but a passing whisper compared to the passion for us and for our salvation that took Jesus on our behalf to the cross, to the grave, and to the resurrected life. Now that is passion!

It is that passion that calls us to run — unstoppable — the race that God Almighty has marked out for us.

~~~

With those thoughts swirling in my mind, I turned my focus back to the London 2012 games unfolding before me. Team USA was in lane 7.

The start was brilliant. It was clear by the end of the first exchange that both Jamaica and the USA teams had the speed to take the race. Coming out of the second exchange, the USA team was firmly in the lead.

And then the magic began.

The USA lead grew. And it grew more. The third exchange was perfect, and the crowd was going wild, sensing that something monumental was happening. The USA team was flying ahead. Eyes flew from the runners to the clock and back again. Barring some catastrophe, the question was no longer *who* would win. The question now was this: Would the USA beat the world record?

Like the crowd in the stadium, Nick and I and the girls were on our feet cheering them on.

And we watched it happen. Team USA sailed across the finish line in a world-record-smashing 40.82 seconds!

The stadium exploded in uproarious celebration. I was jumping so high my daughters thought I would hit the ceiling.

We'd not only seen four amazing individual runners set the world's fastest speed for this race, but we'd also seen a unified team pass the baton with perfect precision and carry it first across the finish line faster than any team in history! And here is a shocking statistic: That unified team of four completed their 400 meters a full 6.78 seconds faster than the individual women's world record for the 400-meter dash. That record is held by Marita Koch of East Germany at 47.60 seconds.[4] Yes, four champion runners collaborating in the relay are faster than a lone champion runner. That's the power of a team.

Perfect collaboration, each runner doing her personal best, running in sync, reaching, receiving, releasing, and pressing on with every ounce of strength she had to give. And when the anchor runner crossed the finish line, she carried not only the baton — she carried her entire team, her entire nation, to the gold.

I love the quote from Tianna Madison, the USA starter that day. "I knew that the Olympic record was coming down," she said. "I just knew that if we had clean baton passes that we would challenge the world record. Smash it like we did? I had no idea. But I knew it was in us."

Wow. Did you catch her phrase "if we had clean baton passes"? It shows exactly what we've been discussing. Everything hinges on what happens in the exchange zone. There we receive the baton, and there we release what is no longer ours to carry so the next runners can play their part. Miss, drop, or fumble the exchange, and the whole team suffers. But if we receive and release the right baton at the right time, victory at the finish line awaits.

Tianna was confident that if her team got the exchange right, they'd win the race and beat the world record. "I knew it was in us," she declared.

I know it's "in us" to do the same! We too can be unstoppable as we run our part in the divine relay.

Why? Because God is *in* us. God is *for* us. And that is what makes us unstoppable. He tells us so in the book of Romans:

> *Those he predestined, he also called; those he called, he also justified; those he justified, he also glorified. What, then, shall we say in response to these things? If God is for us, who can be against us?*
>
> ROMANS 8:30 – 31

Our great God has not left us on our own to muddle through our spiritual lives — our spiritual exchange zones — untrained. His Word and his story, written into you and me and into the lives of all believers the world over, are filled with the wisdom to train us to successfully master our exchange zones and win the race.

The race marked out for *us*.

The race marked out for *you*.

YOUR RACE

Uh-oh. It just got personal, didn't it?

God works that way.

Maybe you are just like me. I settled in to watch a great Olympic race, and the next thing I knew, *WHAM*. All the lights and cameras and eyeballs seemed to swivel from the track to focus squarely on me — on *my* race, *my* baton, *my* exchange zones. And now, in the pages of this book, they focus on you. *Your* race. *Your* baton. *Your* exchange zones.

If you are tempted to question your role in this race out of fear, a sense of inadequacy, or the impression that you've already put in your time and it's someone else's race now, think again.

Are you not an athlete? It doesn't matter.

Are you still warming up? Get moving! The race has already begun.

God has plucked you out of eternity, positioned you in time, and given you gifts and talents to serve him in *this* generation. Your race is now. This is your time in history. You've been handed the baton of faith and entrusted to carry it forward as you run your part in God's divine relay.

Unlike the Olympic Games, the race we run — this divine relay — isn't limited to only a few finalists with millions of spectators. In the divine relay, *every* believer is called to run, and the only spectators are those already in heaven's grandstand. Our race isn't confined to a 400-meter track; it covers all the earth. It started before we got here and will continue after we are gone, so jump in and grasp your baton and run.

Or perhaps you are already running your race and loving it, like I am. Then you know the joys and the challenges of refining your run, growing stronger, and perfecting the handoff.

Have you run out of steam? Are you winded or limping? Don't give up. Keep moving forward.

Have you dropped your baton? Don't walk off the field! You have not been disqualified. Your race isn't over yet.

Have you stumbled or fallen? Have you hit daunting obstacles? Do not stop! Why? Because the Christian life isn't a one-person race. It's a relay. You are not alone; you're part of a team assembled by our unstoppable God to achieve his eternal purposes.

No matter where you are in the race at this point, God is committed to grow you into a champion. You are never limited to your own strength and power. The strength and power of our everlasting God is ready to be unleashed in you!

Come with me through these pages to discover how you can be unstoppable as you master the exchange zone and win the race you were born to win. For we serve an unstoppable God who empowers every believer — that means *you* — with his Holy Spirit.

There is one thing you are responsible for. Only one thing matters: *Run the race marked out for you.* Run forward toward the finish line with every ounce of strength in you and with your eyes fixed on Jesus, so that you too can one day say:

> *I have fought the good fight, I have finished the race, I have kept the faith.*
>
> 2 TIMOTHY 4:7

CHAPTER 2

IMPOSSIBLE IS GOD'S STARTING POINT

The musical tones of Kalli's ringing cell phone startled her awake at 3:00 a.m.

"Hello. A21. This is Kalli."

"I have escaped from the house! I ran away!" the frantic voice of a young woman cried into the phone. "I am hiding. Please come and get me!"

The young woman's broken Greek told Kalli that this victim, like most of the trafficked girls Kalli worked with through The A21 Campaign, had been brought to Kalli's town of Thessaloniki, Greece, from another country. From the sound of her accent, Kalli thought the young woman was likely from Eastern Europe.

"We will help you," Kalli assured her in soothing tones. "What is your name? Where are you?"

"Katja. I am Katja. Come get me fast, please. They must know by now that I am gone and if they find me, they will kill me. They will *kill* me!" The panic in Katja's voice had Kalli's heart racing.

What horrors has this girl been through? God, help me help her, Kalli silently prayed as she thought through how to calm the girl.

"I remember you, Katja," Kalli said, willing her voice to be calm. "We met just two days ago, right? I am so glad you kept my number. I will call my team and get someone to you right away. We will keep you safe. Take a deep breath and tell me where you are."

Katja described her location. It sounded as if she was well hidden at the moment, and she saw no evidence that the traffickers were nearby.

"Lord, hide Katja in the shelter of your wings until we arrive," Kalli prayed aloud, hoping the prayer might calm both of them. This wasn't the first time Kalli had received a panicked call from a young woman whose life was in danger; her emotions always spun wildly at the realization that a human life was at stake — and that she, Kalli, had a part to play in saving it.

"Katja, my team will come right away. But first I must hang up to call them. Can I do that? I will call you back within minutes. Is it okay to call you back at this number? Will you be able to safely answer it?"

There was a pause.

Kalli knew from experience that Katja would fear she was being deceived. Each of the rescued girls found it hard to trust. Who could blame them? Trust had brought most of them to Greece, and that trust had been betrayed. Many of the girls had been promised jobs or education by people they trusted, people they believed to be friends or legitimate recruiters. Most had been told that if they left their homes, paid their money, and traveled with these recruiters to Greece, jobs and other opportunities awaited them. Yet on their arrival, their papers had been taken from them and they'd been brutally beaten and repeatedly raped, threatened with death or the deaths of their families back home, and imprisoned by well-organized traffickers who forced them into prostitution.

"How do I know," Katja's now suspicious voice asked the question Kalli anticipated, "that you will come and take me to safety? How do I know you will not sell me?"

"Katja, you can trust me. I am part of A21. This is what we do. We help girls like you. You met me. You must have trusted me enough to call. Trust me now. Let me hang up and send someone to get you, and I will call you back and help bring you to safety. I promise."

"Yes. But please hurry." Katja hung up.

Kalli felt the weight of the responsibility she now carried. *Lord, you've brought Katja this far. Help us reach her in time!* Kalli prayed, as her trembling fingers dialed the team member who would work with the authorities and make this dangerous drive.

Kalli was running her race, passionately doing her part on the front lines of a brutal war waged by organized crime.

She'd been running it for over three years. This day, God had awakened her at 3:00 a.m. to hand her a new baton — the responsibility to do her part to save Katja's life. Kalli was on point. She was in the exchange zone, already running, reaching with hand outstretched, when that baton landed in her hand. Now she had to run with it.

Kalli was ready. But she remembered well when she hadn't felt ready at all. Three years earlier, Kalli thought it was impossible for her to make a difference in the daunting evil of human trafficking. But this day, knowing that helping Katja meant endangering her own life and the lives of her teammates, Kalli was ready to run this leg of the race marked out for her.

ARE YOU READY TO RUN?

Ready is a tricky word when it comes to following Jesus and doing his will. Why? Because there is a huge difference between *feeling* ready and actually *being* ready.

Did Moses feel ready to return to Egypt and tell Pharaoh to let his people go? No. It seemed an impossible mission. Did Gideon feel ready to go strike down the Midianites and save Israel? No. Did Jeremiah feel ready to be a prophet to the nations? No. Did young Mary, a virgin teenager, feel ready to carry the Son of God in her womb? No. God's Word records the accounts of their questions, protests, reservations, and pleas demonstrating that they didn't feel ready.[5]

In fact, we can go through the Bible page by page and find person after person who didn't *feel* ready to do what God called them to do. But God didn't ask them whether they *felt* ready. He decided they *were* ready. Then he called them and told them what to do. Those we now call heroes of the faith are the ones who obeyed God's call even when they did not feel ready.

God knew he had prepared them. He knew he would provide whatever they needed. He knew what he was going to accomplish through them even though his plans seemed impossible by human standards. So he called them and sent them. We can be certain of this: when God calls us and sends us, we *are* ready, whether we feel we are or not.

How ready are you to join the race and live in the exchange zone, arm outstretched in anticipation of the next baton God has for you?

Don't misunderstand. I'm not asking whether you're ready to fight human trafficking. That's Kalli's lane and mine. Your lane, your baton, may be entirely different. You may be called to care for an aging parent, or to steer a troubled teen through a tumultuous time, or to lead your family through a financial crisis. You may see the need to organize a local food pantry. Perhaps a neighbor is caught in an abusive relationship and needs your help, or a spouse is suffering from depression, or the local elementary school has appealed for after-school mentors for children who have no one at home to read to them or help them with their homework.

Maybe you've become increasingly aware, during your daily commute, of the homeless on the streets of your city, or you feel an inner nudge to volunteer for the youth ministry at your church. Or maybe you went to visit a loved one in prison and saw the loneliness and hopelessness of those who had no visitors. Perhaps your spouse is being transferred to another city and you face the unwelcome need to relocate your family. Is there a pressing social issue you feel that your company, or your church, should be addressing? Do you sense a growing desire to invest less of your time in the career you've been developing for decades and more of your time in compassionate work with those who don't even have a job, much less a career?

The point is, God's call comes to each of us in every age and stage of life. He calls us to step out of our comfort zone and into the exchange zone, ready to run for him and carry the love of God and the truth of his power into the lives of others. Often, we have no idea what task the Lord will assign us until it is thrust into our hands.

My question is, are you ready and willing to run *your* race in the divine relay? To grasp and run with your baton *whatever* it is and *wherever* it takes you?

~~~~~~

God knew Kalli was ready to run her part in the divine relay.

How do I know? Because while I was running *my* race, God placed Kalli in the exchange zone in *my* lane, in A21, and I knew that I was to pass the baton — responsibilities to be carried out at our Thessaloniki safe house — to her.

Of course, Kalli wasn't running alone in this work. Was she the driver who would pick Katja up? No. Was she the police officer who would arrest Katja's traffickers? No. Was she the lawyer who would put Katja on the stand to convict those traffickers, thereby protecting other girls from being stolen, beaten, raped, imprisoned, and enslaved? No. All of those people were further down the track, positioned in their own exchange zones, where God had placed them. Kalli's part in the divine relay was to carry the baton to them.

But before she stepped into the exchange zone at the age of forty-one, Kalli, a homemaker and mother of two children, assumed it was impossible for God to use her to save lives. "I'd been a Christian for about eighteen years, attending church, growing in my faith," Kalli said. "I'd been invited by a friend to attend a Christian women's conference. There I heard Christine tell how God had recently called her into the fight against human trafficking, leading her and her husband, Nick, to start A21. The numbers she revealed were staggering."

They still are. Billions of dollars exchange hands every year in this barbaric business, largely controlled by organized crime around the globe.[6] About 800,000 people are trafficked across international borders every year, and 99 percent of those people never escape.[7]

Kalli said she knew she couldn't just ignore those needs. *But I'm only one woman*, she thought, *a mom with two kids of my own. What can I do about this massive global problem?*

"But there was Christine Caine, this petite little bundle of passionate energy, and she told us that God had called her to help abolish human slavery in the twenty-first century, and that she needed help to do it.

"That seemed impossible. Her goal was so audacious it was almost laughable. I couldn't imagine how I could make a difference, but I sensed God telling me, 'Kalli, you have a part to play in A21.' I knew I couldn't walk away. So, without a clue as to how I could help, I asked God to use me in whatever way he could, and I signed up as a volunteer."

Kalli joined A21 as one of the first volunteers when it began in 2008. She's been unstoppable ever since.

"I had been running in the A21 'volunteer's lane' for a while when another baton was passed to me: to come on staff as the shelter manager," Kalli recalled.

Kalli reached out and grasped that baton as well. Because of that, Kalli had met Katya a few days before that 3:00 a.m. phone call and offered her phone number. And when Katya called, Kalli was there to answer.

Impossible for Kalli, a mom and homemaker, to make a difference? Tell that to Katja. When her life hung in the balance, it was Kalli she called. Then a driver came and took her to safety. A home was provided where Katja learned to heal. An officer arrested her traffickers. A lawyer won their convictions. Do you see? Today, Katya is a free woman back in her home country, attending university — not only because Kalli stood ready in the exchange zone and grasped and ran with her baton, but also because an entire team stood ready, hands outstretched, positioned at the right time and the right place to run their parts in the race.

Each of these individuals had at one time believed it was impossible for them to make a difference in a global problem. But they've discovered that together, with each of them carrying their own unique batons, they are unstoppable in carrying out God's plan.

That sounds far too complex to be real, doesn't it?

It sounds impossible.

Fantastic! *Impossible is God's starting point.*

WHAT HOLDS YOU BACK?

Because our God is God of the impossible, the seemingly impossible can't hold us back from achieving God's purposes for us. But other things can. Failure to enter the race or an unwillingness to take our position in the exchange zone will keep us from the thrill of playing our part in God's relay.

So allow me to ask a personal question: What holds you back?

Anything?

Are you 100 percent satisfied that you are engaged in the relay, in the right lane, grasping your baton, running full-out, holding nothing back?

Here is why I ask. I travel the globe talking with Christians in every walk of life and every phase of Christian maturity, and I've discovered that our churches are filled with brothers and sisters who, for a host of reasons, feel dissatisfied with their spiritual condition.

- Some are new believers just beginning to understand the nature, character, and purposes of God. They are eager to run but not sure how to get started.
- Others attend church but are weary or burned out from living a busy or self-focused Christian life without seeing the life change or the world change they long for.
- Some have lost interest in attending church and feel the established church has lost its relevance, but they themselves long to be relevant in the world, to make a difference.
- Most long for a taste of God's power and presence unlike anything they've ever known.
- Many believe they are not qualified or gifted enough to be used by God in big ways.

Did you find yourself in this list? If I missed your description, but you too feel that something is missing in your spiritual life, take a few minutes to articulate the problem. Do it now. Write it in! Because until you can identify your current condition, how can you move forward?

_____

_____

_____

_____

Now that you've identified your current spiritual condition, here's the good news: God has an eternal purpose for the whole body of Christ and a divinely chosen part for every single believer. He has uniquely designed and selected each and every believer to fulfill his or her purpose. I'm going to repeat that, because it's that important.

God has an eternal purpose for the whole body of Christ and a divinely chosen part for every single believer. He has uniquely designed and selected each and every believer to fulfill his or her purpose.

That includes you, my friend. If you seek God's will, if you offer yourself to run his race, he will equip you to join or return to the race, no matter how impossible that may seem. Not only will he equip you as an individual runner for personal spiritual enrichment, but he will also train you as part of an unstoppable team, the church of Jesus Christ. We have been entrusted with the mission of advancing the kingdom of God on the earth. Never underestimate how huge, how mighty, how world-changing and eternity-altering this divine relay really is.

When you step forward, willing to join the race and run, you, like Kalli, will see that the seemingly impossible — you making a difference in this world — isn't impossible at all. God has empowered you with his very own Holy Spirit to run to win.

Just the other day Kalli wrote, "For me, A21 is not a job — it is my passion! It is my life! I love every moment of it, even the most challenging parts. I never in my wildest dreams imagined that I would play a part in saving lives. I am so honored to be where I am today."

I'm with Kalli! When Nick and I started The A21 Campaign, I had no idea where it would take me. I did not realize how many legs to this relay there were. I keep handing off more and more batons with every new office that opens and every gathering I address; and now, so many others are running that more batons are in the relay than ever. The surprise of this divine relay is that just when you think you've finished your leg of the race, you discover that the best part is still ahead, that God had so much more in mind for you than you ever imagined. The ride is so wild and thrilling that the more I run, the more my passion grows to run even more. If you don't have a spiritual passion burning inside you today, challenging you, leaving you wowed and honored to be doing your work for the Lord, you're missing the thrill of running your part in the race. If that's the case, then please work through this book with a seeking, open heart and an outstretched, open hand.

Don't even wait for the end of the book. Pray now!

Oh Lord, sign me up for my part in the divine relay. Start with my "impossible." Place me in my lane, in my position, in my exchange zone. Lord, I reach out, palm open, to receive the baton you have for me. Fuel me with your passion, Lord, and I will run!

Amen?
Amen!

DECISION TIME

If you just prayed that prayer with me and are awaiting your first baton — or if you've been running for a while and have a baton in hand or are waiting for the next one — here are a few questions to help you become unstoppable while living in the exchange zone.

- Why do I hold back from running my race with 100 percent commitment?
- Why do I sometimes fail to receive the baton that God holds out to me?
- What do I do with my reluctance to release the baton — given that, when I depend on others, they sometimes let me down or fail me?

- What makes me fumble the exchange or drop the baton? And if I do, what then?
- What happens if I run off course, and how can I find my way back?
- What is it that tempts me to quit the race altogether?
- The race is sometimes long and hard. Why does my passion sometimes wither away, and what can I do to refuel it?
- What can I do to run better, smarter, and stronger?

We will explore the answers to these questions in the chapters to come, so that when we hit such questions, challenges, and obstacles, they won't stop us in our tracks. We'll be prepared and equipped, unstoppable in our commitment to run the race marked out for us.

Here is a news flash: We don't have to look any further than our own neighborhoods or even our own homes to find the glaring needs of our broken world. There are people who need to know they are loved, children in need of hope and help, teens suffering from loneliness and depression, coworkers who don't know the truth and freedom of the gospel, friends caught in destructive life choices, elderly who need to know they are valued and honored. The list is endless.

Yet somehow, far too many of us reason this way: I don't know where my calling is. I don't feel led. Not yet.

I confess, I get a little over-the-top passionate in my answer to that, but here it is:

WAKE UP, CHRISTIAN!

God's Word calls you. Let God's Word lead you.

This is why it is said: "Wake up, sleeper, rise from the dead, and Christ will shine on you." Be very careful, then, how you live — not as unwise but as wise, making the most of every opportunity, because the days are evil.

EPHESIANS 5:14–16

Always give yourselves fully to the work of the Lord, because you know that your labor in the Lord is not in vain.

1 CORINTHIANS 15:58

Do you want to find your place? Do you want to know your part in bringing light and hope and healing into this fractured world?

Do something.

Do anything.

But don't just stand there.

Run!

Pray. Fast. Find a need that needs filling and fill it. Find others who are running and run with them. Ask God to move your heart and open your eyes to those other runners who might hand off batons to you. Just find one thing to do and get started.

God Almighty, who calls you by name, wants to make you a partner in his eternal work. He invites us to be world-changers by sharing the good news of eternal life and caring for the needs of a broken, hurting world. That's what running the race marked out for you is all about.

You've heard Kalli's passion and mine. Doing God's work leaves us wanting to do more. As we see lives changing through our efforts, as we see God start with the impossible and go on to change the world with the baton we are carrying, our passion to play our part in his divine relay grows even stronger.

Today, when Kalli looks at Katja and sees a young woman who has learned that God loves her and who has experienced deep healing, Kalli sees how God is using her to change the world. When she sees that Katja has forgiven the traffickers who deceived, brutalized, and enslaved her, Kalli stands amazed. Because of Kalli's willingness to run her race, something seemingly impossible is now unfolding in Katja's heart.

The same will be true for you. When you run your race, you

will see the impossible melt away as God's power is unleashed in you and through you to a broken world. God's plans for your eternal impact on this world are beyond your wildest imagination.

Sound impossible? Of course it is!

But impossible is God's starting point.

Jesus looked at them and said, "With man this is impossible, but with God all things are possible."

MATTHEW 19:26

CHAPTER 3

FULLY QUALIFIED FOR YOUR RACE

The impossible was God's starting point for Kalli's work to save trafficked women.

But her work with A21 was not the beginning of her *race*, just the beginning of her A21 *leg* in the race. You want to hear about impossible? Listen to the story of how God's ongoing divine relay through the ages brought Kalli into her race and how seemingly unqualified she and her forerunners were for the parts they were about to play in the grand race.

Kalli grew up in South Africa. Rejected by her mother as a child, Kalli was sexually and physically abused for many years, which eventually led, at the age of eighteen, to her accepting a job in her city of Cape Town, South Africa, as an escort for her company's clients, understanding full well that providing sex was part of her job. And guess what her father did for a living? He was part of the Mafia in South Africa — a drug dealer, a nightclub owner, and a trafficker of humans. Haunted by childhood traumas and a broken family, starving for affection, and feeling used and worthless, Kalli sought to escape her pain through drug abuse.

This is the woman who, in chapter 2, answered the desperate call from Katja. Do you believe this? I couldn't make this stuff up!

Something changed that drastically altered the course of Kalli's life. Her father — a drug-dealing human trafficker — accepted Christ. He had a total God encounter, and with it came a dramatic life change. God's call to Kalli's father, and his acceptance of that call, led him to carry the baton of faith into Kalli's life, where it multiplied. After witnessing the radical change in her father's life, Kalli surrendered her own life to Jesus and became a Christian at the age of twenty-three.

Kalli joined a church, and, thanks to the influence of church leaders and teachers who were doing their part in the divine relay, she began to run her race. This brought her to the point of stepping into the spiritual exchange zone of wanting to be used by God to help others. One exchange zone led to the next, one baton to the next, and so she was running in the exchange zone when, at the age of forty-one, she reached out and grasped the A21 baton.

Now let's step back and consider the one who brought the gospel to Kalli's father. We don't know his name, but God does. And of course there was someone who carried the gospel to that person, and the person before. While we don't know their stories, their qualifications, their sins, their flaws and obstacles and struggles, we do know that one after another, they each stepped into their own exchange zone, received the baton of faith, and passed it forward until it landed in Kalli's outstretched hand. Do you see how the divine relay stretches back?

And now Katja — a once broken and abused sex slave — having received the baton from Kalli, is running her own race, carrying on the baton. To whom will she carry it? We can only imagine, but God knows. Katja is one of many girls who've been helped through Kalli's work at A21. They have all moved forward, many of them coming to faith and carrying their batons as well. Some are carrying their batons in Greece. Others are in Bulgaria, Nigeria, the US, Australia, South Africa, the UK, Norway, the Ukraine, and Asia.

Do you see how the divine relay stretches forward? Are you beginning to get the picture of how big, how huge, how interconnected and unstoppable it is? Each runner's efforts are multiplied many times over. Each handoff opens limitless possibilities for future handoffs that spin off in multiple directions, carrying God's work across the globe in ways we could never imagine. God's Word describes the unstoppable, ongoing nature of the divine relay, touching generation after generation with these words:

> One generation commends your works to another; they tell of your mighty acts.... All your works praise you, Lord; your faithful people extol you. They tell of the glory of your kingdom and speak of your might, so that all people may know of your mighty acts and the glorious splendor of your kingdom. Your kingdom is an everlasting kingdom, and your dominion endures through all generations.
>
> PSALM 145:4, 10–13

Wow! What a privilege God gives to you and me to play our part in this ageless saga.

THE MULTIPLICATION FACTOR

When we move into the exchange zone, ready to accept the baton God has in store for us, God multiplies our efforts. This divine multiplication factor is critically important for us to understand. Why? Because all too often, rather than seeing ourselves as qualified by God to play a great part in his race, we look at our lives — our limitations, our meager resources, our brokenness, our apparent insignificance in this huge world — and rather than moving boldly into the exchange zone, we feel unqualified to be used mightily by God, and so we slink to the sidelines.

But the race isn't run from the sidelines! The Christian life is no spectator sport. It is heartbreaking for me to meet Christians who love the Lord and desire to serve him, but who shy away from playing their part because they don't understand God's divine multiplication factor. How tempting to look at our broken world and messy lives and falsely believe we are too broken, the pain is too much, the evil of this world is too entrenched, for us to make a difference. Countless believers are stopped dead in their tracks before they even make it to their first exchange zone. "After all," they reason, "I'm just one person. My involvement isn't going to make a dent in what's wrong in this world. I'm not qualified enough for God to use me in important ways."

That kind of thinking would have stopped the man in South Africa from witnessing to the Mafia, drug-dealing human-trafficker who was Kalli's father. That kind of thinking would have kept that radically changed father from sharing his faith with his wounded daughter, Kalli. That kind of thinking would have stopped his daughter, the former drug-addicted prostitute, from volunteering for A21 and eventually coming on staff as the shelter manager. So who would have befriended Katja and given her a number to call? Who would have answered the phone at 3:00 a.m.? Would her trafficker still be in business, stealing other young lives, rather than behind bars like he is today? Do you see the potential ripple effects when just one person walks away from his or her exchange zone? This is what happens when, believing we are unqualified to make a difference, we choose not to live in the exchange zone.

Of course we are small, but God is huge.

Of course we have limitations, but God is limitless.

Of course we are weak, but God is strong.

Of course we are finite, but God is infinite.

Of course we are imperfect, but God is perfect.

Of course we fail, but God never fails.

Of course we can choose to stop, but God is unstoppable. And if we choose to carry the batons he brings our way, we will witness how he gladly multiplies our efforts and makes us and our impact on this world unstoppable.

God calls you to step into the exchange zone not because *you* are mighty and strong. He calls you to take your place in the race because *he* is mighty and strong, and he plans to accomplish his work in you and through you!

HOW NOT ENOUGH BECOMES MORE THAN ENOUGH

Some two thousand years ago, on a hillside swarming with thousands of hungry people, the disciples found themselves confronted with a problem that looked too big to overcome. Watch what unfolded as God multiplied what was offered to him. And look for how God speaks to you about running your race.

Jesus had been teaching and healing a large crowd all day.[8] His words were so life-giving, so earth-shattering, that the people stayed hour after hour after hour to hear more. Late in the day, the disciples came to Jesus, saying he should send the people away so they could go to surrounding villages and buy themselves something to eat.

So Jesus asks, "How many loaves do you have?"

Andrew, one of the disciples, comes back with, "Here is a boy with five small barley loaves and two small fish, but how far will they go among so many?" Notice that Andrew didn't just say it was five barley loaves and two fish. He called them *small* loaves and *small* fish, as if he wanted to emphasize that such a small amount was insignificant in light of the huge need.

Notice that Jesus asks them how much there is to go around. He makes sure that the disciples recognize the limitations they are facing. Often it is when we come face-to-face with our limitations that we give up, thinking all is lost. But when we recognize our limitations, then we also recognize when God demonstrates his limitless power. Until we hit our limit, we often assume we can provide, we can deliver, and we can produce.

What are you facing today that brings you face-to-face with your limitations, leaving you questioning how qualified you are to make a difference in this broken world? Is it a broken past? A dream that has died? A lack of time, money, education, leadership skills, influence, or confidence? We must never assess a difficulty in light of our own resources but in light of God's resources. You can step boldly into the exchange zone not because you have no limits (we all have plenty!) but because *God's resources are limitless*. Jesus accepted the five loaves and two fishes, small though they were. One packed lunch. A meager amount of food. It was all the boy had, but he offered it all. If the boy had kept his little lunch, it would have remained little. If you keep your little, it will remain little as well. But if you step into the exchange zone ready to offer what little you have to be used by God in moving the baton forward, your little will be multiplied as you run.

When the boy gave his little to Jesus, Jesus blessed it, and it became much in his hands. It is never about how little we have. It is about what our little has the potential to become in the hands of a miracle-working God. Don't focus on what you don't have, what you can't do, what isn't enough. Just offer your "not enough" to God, and he will multiply it into *more* than enough. That's what happens when you are living in the exchange zone, offering yourself to be used by God.

I love this next part! Do you know the first thing Jesus did with that meager offering? He looked up to heaven and gave thanks to God for the little he was given by the boy. I wonder what it was like for that boy to see his meager meal held up to the heavens by the hands of a grateful Jesus. Jesus, of course, knew it wasn't going to remain little, that it was about to be multiplied into great abundance. But let's not miss this moment. The Son of God, holding our offering up to Almighty God and blessing it with his thanks! Remember Kalli, unable to imagine what she could possibly do to help but volunteering anyway? We need to be like her. We don't need to know *how* God is going to use our meager offering. We only need to know that he *wants* to use it. Always remember that *God celebrates our gifts to him and blesses them.*

Next, Jesus broke the bread and the fish. When he blessed it, there were five and two. But when he broke it, we lose count. The more Jesus broke the bread and fish, the more there was to feed and nourish. The disciples started distributing the food, and soon what was broken was feeding thousands. *The miracle is in the breaking.* It is in the breaking that God multiplies not enough into more than enough.

Are there broken places in your life so painful that you fear the breaking will destroy you? Do you come from a broken home? Did you have a broken marriage? Did you have a broken past? Have you experienced brokenness in your body? Have your finances been broken? You may think your brokenness has disqualified you from being able to run in the divine relay, but as with my own life and Kalli's, when we give God our brokenness, it qualifies us to be used by God to carry a baton of hope, restoration, and grace to others on the sidelines who are broken. What should have disqualified Kalli from the race was the very thing that qualified her for it.

Put your broken pieces into God's hands and watch him use them to work his wonders. Some of the most life-giving people I have met have gone through something that broke them and allowed them to see God use for his glory that which the enemy meant for evil. *When our broken pieces are offered to God, he multiplies them for his purposes.*

Not only was there enough for everyone to have their fill, there were leftovers! Listen to what Jesus said when everyone had been filled and satisfied:

> *He said to his disciples, "Gather the pieces that are left over. Let nothing be wasted."*
>
> JOHN 6:12

Did you hear Jesus' words? "Let nothing be wasted." So precious to the Lord are our offerings, our broken pieces, that even when he's multiplied them into an overabundance, he puts every bit of it to good use. The next time you are tempted to withhold your contribution to the kingdom, believing it to be too small or too broken to make a difference, don't forget that not only will God celebrate, bless, and multiply your contribution, he will also value every little bit of it. *God never wastes what we offer to him.*

All four of the disciples who wrote the Gospels — Matthew, Mark, Luke, and John — record this miraculous hillside feeding, and all report the number of people fed as five thousand men, which did not include the women and children. Matthew 14:21 makes that very clear: "The number of those who ate was about five thousand men, besides women and children."

Have you ever noticed that part of the verse? I used to think, *Why didn't they count everybody? Why only the men?* Until a powerful realization occurred to me.

Whose lunch was it that Jesus multiplied? It was a child who gave his meager lunch — an *uncounted* boy! The disciples did not count the very one whom God had moved into position to release his miracle.

Isn't that just like God to use people whom other people do not count?

You may think you are too insignificant to count when it comes to God handing off batons. But God counts you. He more than counts you. God counts *on* you. *The uncounted count.* You matter.

As a mom, I like to think about that boy's mama who packed his lunch that day. There she was, doing her mom thing, packing ordinary foods. She didn't know she was packing the ingredients for a miracle, did she? I wonder if she was in the crowd that day. Did she see what God did with those ordinary ingredients? Or did she hear about it from her wide-eyed son and neighbors later that night? Either way, she must have been amazed that it was her common food that was miraculously multiplied.

Are you holding back from stepping boldly into the exchange zone because you have nothing extraordinary to offer? God is not waiting for you, hoping you'll eventually bring him extraordinary talents, abilities, accomplishments, and gifts. The time is now to give him what you have, no matter how ordinary or insignificant it seems. In the divine relay, *God uses ordinary to do the extraordinary.*

GREAT EXPECTATIONS

There's no reason to hold back, lingering on the sidelines rather than expectantly taking your position in the exchange zone. Be confident that God will take your little and make it much.

Are your resources too limited to change the world? Great. His resources are limitless. Do you not have enough to offer him? No problem. God multiplies your not enough into more than enough.

Do you doubt the value of your contribution, wondering what you could possibly do to help in God's kingdom work? Offer yourself joyfully, knowing that God celebrates your gifts to him and blesses them, no matter how meager.

Are you broken, thinking you are too wounded to be qualified to serve? The miracle is in the breaking. What has been broken, God is able to multiply for his purposes.

Do you feel so used up and worn down that all you have left to offer are your leftovers? Marvelous. God values your leftovers and never wastes one morsel of what you have to offer.

Do you believe you are too insignificant to count in carrying batons that will change this world and have an eternal impact? The uncounted count. God counts on you doing your part.

Are you so ordinary that you have no remarkable gifts or talents for God to use? How wonderful! God uses the ordinary to do his extraordinary.

Congratulations! You've passed the test. Your "not enough" becomes more than enough when you take your place in the exchange zone, arm outstretched, ready to receive the next baton God will place in your open palm. You've qualified to take your place in the exchange zone.

Each of you should use whatever gift you have received to serve others, as faithful stewards of God's grace in its various forms. If anyone speaks, they should do so as one who speaks the very words of God. If anyone serves, they should do so with the strength God provides, so that in all things God may be praised through Jesus Christ. To him be the glory and the power for ever and ever. Amen.

1 PETER 4:10–11

CHAPTER 4

EMBRACE YOUR PLACE

The Friday night crowd at the youth center where I served a few nights a week seemed larger than usual. The place hummed with boisterous conversations, loud music, and the constant motion of teenagers and young adults mixing with one another and with the staff. I spotted Jeremy coming my way through the crowd. He was a regular. I didn't know his story, but he had all the telltale signs of a lonely, troubled kid in search of a place to belong. Caring for him and the hundreds like him had become my passion.

I was twenty-two years old and had been volunteering at the youth center for several months, serving food to hurting and broken young people, listening to their problems, and inviting them to tell me their stories. Coming here was the highlight of my week, and I loved knowing that each time I showed up, I was making a difference in the life of a lonely or wounded person. I was such a regular volunteer that I'd become a team coordinator and was on duty that night. Maybe this was the night I'd find out more of Jeremy's story.

"Jeremy," I called out to him. "Over here." I waved him over.

His head turned at the sound of my voice, and when our eyes met, I could see he was drunk. He staggered over to me and stood there for a moment, swaying a little. His color looked bad, and before I had the chance to say another word, he clutched his stomach and then — excuse me for being so graphic — he projectile vomited all over the people in his path, me included.

My leadership skills flew into action, and instinctively I did what a leader does — I delegated. As I steadied Jeremy and led him toward a chair, I turned to one of my team and said, "Go get some toilet paper and clean this mess up."

A moment later a few people came back, rolls of toilet paper in hand, and I was about to issue my next instructions when suddenly I felt the Holy Spirit saying to me, "Christine, you wipe up the vomit."

I have an extreme aversion to dealing with vomit, even to this day with my own children. But my sense of God's presence was so palpable that my heart started racing. I reached for a roll of toilet paper and began wiping the vomit off of Jeremy's chin and jacket and shirt. As I did, a tenderness for him rose up inside of me, and I sensed the Holy Spirit impressing on my heart, "Christine, this is what you're going to spend your life doing — wiping up the vomit of a lost and broken generation."

I was so new to running in the divine relay that hearing from God in such a powerful way made me tremble with awe. As others backed away from the sight and smell of this mess, I got Jeremy cleaned up, then began wiping the floor. I knew this was a profound moment between God and me. I was on holy ground. I was responding to the call of God, realizing that this messy work was his holy work.

I admit it. Before that day, wiping up vomit wouldn't have been on my short list of important work for God. But that was then. Today I know better than to think we can rank the importance or status of the work God calls us to do. The Lord has taught me that when we run the race he has marked out for us, he chooses which batons he passes to us. He places us in the right lane and chooses which position we are to take within that lane. Every leg of the race is preparation for the legs to come. He knows the perfect timing to promote us from one baton to the next, one lane to the next, one position to the next; and such promotions oftentimes don't look like we expected them to look. That day with Jeremy, I was promoted from coordinating staff to wiping vomit, and in accepting that promotion, I'd moved closer to the heart of God.

As I was wiping vomit from the floor on my hands and knees, God was giving me my first lesson in a critically important principle: In order to thrive in the exchange zone, we must learn to *embrace our place.* To embrace your place means that wherever you are in life, no matter what season you are in or what circumstances you face, you see yourself as an important member of God's divine relay, and you accept and do God's will today in light of his plan for all eternity.

In principle, that sounds simple, doesn't it? But in reality — in those covered-in-vomit kinds of moments — it is all too easy for us to miss the opportunities to embrace our place and so miss the opportunities to accept the next baton God is bringing our way.

ONE TEAM, MANY RUNNERS

Today, Nick and I have the opportunity to build the local church throughout the world. The church is rich in its diversity of worship expressions, culture, tradition, music styles, people, programs, and passions. How boring it would be if everyone was the same and this earth saw only one single expression of God's greatness. No one denomination, tradition, tribe, or church, and no one ministry, task, mission, or work displays all of God's greatness any more than one star reflects all the glory of God. Together we reflect more of God than any of us can do alone.

To help us understand this mystery, God chose the image of the human body.

Now you are the body of Christ, and each one of you is a part of it.

1 CORINTHIANS 12:27

God calls us the body of Christ, and he chooses to be represented on this earth through us, his body. People see God at work on the earth through his church. The body of Christ is the visible representation of an invisible God to our friends, our neighbors, and the world. The more connected, interdependent, and unified we are, the more of God the world sees through the work of his church. He wants to work through us to impact the world now and in the generations to come. Look at this next passage and ask yourself how it applies to you as you run your part in God's divine relay.

Just as a body, though one, has many parts, but all its many parts form one body, so it is with Christ. For we were all baptized by one Spirit so as to form one body — whether Jews or Gentiles, slave or free — and we were all given the one Spirit to drink. Even so the body is not made up of one part but of many.

1 CORINTHIANS 12:12 – 14

When the church is unified, working together like a healthy body, then we have the capacity to make God known to those around us, and we depict a big, unstoppable God who is able to do big things on the earth. Conversely, if the church is disjointed, divided, or broken, then we will depict a small God to our world. Every muscle, limb, organ, sinew, tissue, and ligament is crucial, or God would not have put it there.

Do you see that there are no insignificant parts of the body? Each one has its own purpose and contributes to the body's functioning as a healthy, vibrant, whole living organism. This was brought home to me years ago when my anterior cruciate ligament (ACL) snapped in a skiing accident. With my ACL no longer in its place, my knee was not stable. Because my knee was weak, it could not bear the weight of my leg. This in turn could not hold up my body, which affected everything else I tried to do. Because this one ligament was not in place, I was required to wear a leg brace. This made my left side compensate for the weakness in my right side. It was not until I had surgery on my right knee and then strengthened the muscles surrounding that knee that I could again walk freely and my right side could bear its share of my body weight.

Now think about the women's relay team that won the gold in the London 2012 Olympic Games. Who do you think determined which woman would be the starter and which would be runners two and three and the anchor? The coach made that decision. The coach assessed the greatest strengths and greatest potential of each runner and purposefully chose their positions — their place — on the field. Was the starter more important than the anchor? Or the second runner greater than the third? No. The team's success was dependent on each of the four embracing her place and doing her part. Only then could the team win the gold.

DISPLACED OR MISPLACED

If we are going to run this race well, we must each learn to embrace our place — the place and position in God's divine relay that he has chosen for us. Sadly, I often receive emails and letters from Christians all over the world who, for one reason or another, feel displaced or misplaced in the body of Christ. In addition, as Nick and I travel to churches around the globe, we are often called on to help churches and individuals work through challenges and barriers in embracing their part in the work they do for the Lord. How about you? Have you found yourself mystified, frustrated, or discouraged when the reality of playing your part in serving God falls short of your expectations?

No doubt there are a myriad of reasons why people reach the point of confusion, frustration, discouragement, and apparent dead ends when they are running their race. That is to be expected. Working with broken people in a broken world will always bring challenges. But if these challenges are not addressed, they can become barriers to running well or threats that send runners off the track entirely. So let's take the time to recognize a few common causes of feeling displaced or misplaced.

Obscurity and Anonymity

Many believers feel stuck behind the scenes where they work diligently without much in the way of thanks or recognition. Others feel lost in obscurity, believing the work they are doing for God is too small to make a difference for him in this world. Some begin doing God's work with the hope of making a difference but then discover that such work is messy, smelly, unglamorous, and tedious. How easy to mistake such work as menial or of little eternal value. Many times people on a short-term missions team leave the comfort of their home church with visions of winning converts to the faith only to find themselves knee-deep in mud, lifting heavy cinder blocks to build a shelter in the shadow and stench of a garbage dump. "Is this what I came for?" they might ask. "Surely God has bigger, more important work for me to do."

Circumstances and Trials

I also speak to many whose challenges are coming from circumstances that thwart their efforts to do what they believe they've been called to do. Maybe adoptive parents who have opened their home to an at-risk child repeatedly find themselves picking up the child from the police station instead of seeing him thrive in the arms of his adoptive family who are offering unconditional love.

Perhaps a young couple wants to begin a family, but they struggle with infertility. Maybe a permit falls through on the expansion of a ministry center, or a woman teaching a thriving neighborhood Bible study is struck down with cancer, or a man leading an effective prison ministry loses his job and must relocate in order to support his family. The list is endless. Add to this list your own unexpected circumstances that, just when you believe you've hit your stride, seem to derail the work you were sure you were called to do.

Promotion and Timing

If I have learned one thing in ministry, it is that most God dreams take longer than we think to realize, cost more than we ever thought we would have to pay, and are far more painful to birth than we ever imagined. Nothing great happens overnight. God works much more like a conventional oven than he does a microwave when he is doing his work in us and through us. Many start the race with high energy and vibrant passion, but when they do not move ahead as quickly as they think they should, they lose their zeal and commitment.

These common challenges can lead some to make a huge mistake: they stop running their race! Some throw in the towel and quit. Some shrink back from taking risks and serve instead within a comfort zone that never stretches them. Others decide to quietly sit in the pew and never serve again, focusing solely on their own private spiritual needs but missing out on the call, the growth, and the rewards of running the race marked out for them.

If you have found yourself in these few paragraphs, know this: God has a specific purpose and place for you. There are no throwaway runners, lanes, legs, or positions in God's divine relay. Every runner is important. Every baton, every lane, every position, and every leg of the race is important.

God not only has a place for each one of us, he also has perfect timing when it comes to moving us from one position to the next. If you leave the race, if you stop running because of disillusionment or disappointment, you will be disconnected from the very purposes God has in mind for you. If you try to transplant yourself to the place you want to be in order to avoid the challenges and hurdles of your current portion of the race, you may find that you are even more frustrated or ineffective than you already were.

But if you stay faithful in your pursuit of God and learn to embrace your place, then his work in and through you will be unstoppable. When you learn to embrace your place, you trust that God has chosen you for a purpose, is preparing you for the future he has planned, has placed you in position for the next leg of your journey, and will, at the right time, hand off the right baton that will accomplish his work in you and through you.

Let's take a closer look at how to grow your trust in God's choice for your place in his race.

GOD CHOOSES THE PART WE PLAY

I don't know what your story is, where you've been, what you've done, or what has been done to you. But I do know from God's Word that you are not here, in this place and this time, by accident. As you give God your time, your gifts, your resources and talents, he will use them to have a critically important and eternal impact on this world.

God demonstrates this truth in the story of David. Through his life, we can see God's preparation process in action and discover the principles we need to grasp so that we, like David, can learn to embrace our place.

Saul was the first king of the Israelites, but after leading them for about twenty-five years, Saul rebelled so much against the Lord that God sent his prophet Samuel to anoint the future king who would succeed Saul.[9]

The Lord said to Samuel ... "I am sending you to Jesse of Bethlehem. I have chosen one of his sons to be king."

1 SAMUEL 16:1

So Samuel went as instructed and had Jesse present his sons. We are about to witness an important principle: *God chooses the part we play.* Let's admit it — from a human standpoint, there are times when God's choices defy our logic. Left to his own judgment, the prophet got it wrong. He looked at the firstborn, Eliab, saw his impressive appearance and size, and assumed Eliab must be God's choice.

When they arrived, Samuel saw Eliab and thought, "Surely the Lord's anointed stands here before the Lord." But the Lord said to Samuel, "Do not consider his appearance or his height, for I have rejected him. The Lord does not look at the things people look at. People look at the outward appearance, but the Lord looks at the heart."

1 SAMUEL 16:6–7

Clearly, God's ways are not our ways. He's not looking for obvious external qualifications. God looks at the heart. So Samuel considered the next son, and then the next, and the one after that, until finally,

Jesse had seven of his sons pass before Samuel, but Samuel said to him, "The Lord has not chosen these." So he asked Jesse, "Are these all the sons you have?"

"There is still the youngest," Jesse answered. "He is tending the sheep."

1 SAMUEL 16:10–11

David, the last born, the least qualified from a human point of view, was so far removed from his father's mind as a possible candidate for this job that Jesse hadn't even brought him to the selection process. A mere teenager, David was out tending the sheep, faithfully serving his family in the job he'd been given. We can hardly imagine his shock when, plucked from his shepherding, he found himself face-to-face with a prophet of God who did this:

> Then the Lord said, "Rise and anoint him; this is the one." So Samuel took the horn of oil and anointed him in the presence of his brothers, and from that day on the Spirit of the Lord came powerfully upon David.
>
> 1 SAMUEL 16:12 – 13

David did not choose to be king. God chose David to be king.

And where was David when he was summoned? Serving in obscurity. When we trust that God chooses the part we play, then we need not worry about our obscurity and anonymity, only our obedience to play our part. Are you given the jobs that no one else wants? Welcome them. Do you feel disregarded by your family, your boss, your coworkers? Then you are in David's good company. He was marked by God as the right person for the right job at the right time. We must remember that God has designed us and knows how and where we fit perfectly into his body so that we will reach our optimum potential. You must have confidence in God's design and placement in order to embrace your place.

If you feel lost in anonymity in the place you are now serving, think of David, working in the fields when his brothers were being paraded in front of Samuel, each as a potential king. You are not anonymous to God. He knows your name. He sees you when you faithfully serve him. God knows your potential and your faithfulness when no one else does. God sees your heart, and if God has assigned you to your place, God will find you when it is time for your promotion.

GOD PREPARES THOSE HE CHOOSES

What we must grasp in learning to embrace our place is that spiritual growth is a process. Destiny is not an instant click and upload.

In today's culture of digital technology, anyone can, in a matter of moments, snap a picture and upload it for instant viewing across the globe. But back in my day, when dinosaurs roamed the earth (at least that's how my girls envision it when I try to explain the old photographic process), photos were developed in a darkroom. Working under the illumination of a special red light, the film image was transferred to paper that then was dipped in several trays of chemical solutions. Photo paper moved from tray to tray, solution to solution, and the image began to slowly emerge. The process took time and care. If someone opened the darkroom door and let in too much light or tried to take shortcuts in the development process, the images would be destroyed. If you wanted great photos, you had to allow the full time for the development process.

In the same way, to fulfill God's purpose for our lives, we must commit to the process of God's darkroom. It is there, over time, that God prepares us for the purposes we will serve. God uses others in the body of Christ plus time, circumstances and trials, and gradual development to burn the light of Christ into our souls so that when we emerge from his darkroom, nothing can destroy the image of his Son developed in our lives.

We see this in David's life. He was a teenager on the day he was anointed to be the future king of Israel. But King Saul was still on the throne with no plans of stepping down. The prophet Samuel had kept his mission a secret, knowing full well that to do otherwise would put his own life, and David's, in danger. Neither Samuel nor David had any inkling of when David would take the throne. I wonder if they could have imagined that about fifteen years would pass before David, at the age of thirty, would be crowned. *Just because David had been anointed with a divine purpose did not mean it was his appointed time.*

As a teenager, David did not yet have the skill, wisdom, or knowledge to lead the nation. He was anointed, but his character and spirit needed to be developed, and that would require that he follow and obey God every step of the way along what would prove to be a long, mystifying, and difficult journey. (Think for a moment of your own long, mystifying, and difficult journey.) God did not inform David of his timetable. He did not map out the journey and discuss it with David. David didn't have a clue as to what was going to unfold that would take him from tending sheep to leading a nation. But as we witness the next fifteen years of David's life, we can see his progression from the fields to the throne room.

In the same way, I didn't have a clue that God's work would take me from a local youth center to a national youth ministry, then to a global church ministry, and then on to be one of God's warriors in the fight against the injustice of human slavery. I never imagined that God would use an adopted, abused, marginalized, minority female (I tell that part of my story in my book *Undaunted*) to open rescue homes for women sold as sex slaves around the world and to hire lawyers to win convictions of the organized criminals exploiting those women. To this day, I stand in awe that God uses me to travel across the globe to beckon believers to take up their batons and run their hearts out for the cause of Jesus Christ.

But I can see now that I didn't need to know any of that. All I needed to do was embrace the place God had for me that day in the youth center, wiping Jeremy's vomit off him, off myself, and off the floor. All I needed to do was be obedient to serve God where he'd placed me that day. All I needed to do was answer God's call to do his work on this earth. The rest was up to him!

David was obedient and embraced his place. He became an

armor-bearer to Saul. Here he practiced humility and learned things about palace life he could not have known tending sheep. Assuming the posture of a servant was his training ground to be a king. He was the errand boy in battle, willingly carrying lunch to his brothers. Even though they'd seen him anointed, he did not seek to lord it over them, but instead, he served them. In fact, God positioned David as a lunch boy at the battlefield at that time for a specific reason, for it was there, as David delivered lunches — a seemingly unimportant act of service — that he heard for himself the taunts of the giant, Goliath.

Had David not spent years protecting his sheep from predators, had he not been learning and meditating on the Scriptures, he would not have had the strength or the courage to take out the giant. All along the way, David proved himself faithful. He did not begrudgingly do what he was asked to do; he did it wholeheartedly and faithfully, no matter the cost.

Are you seeing how God works? Can you see your own life path in light of this principle? God is always preparing us for the next leg in the race, always training us. Sometimes we might know the position God has called us to, but we must remember that timing is everything. Our here and now is God's preparation for our future. This is why we must remain faithful, committed, and loyal, even when we cannot fathom how good can come out of bad. There is a process — a divine order — that requires submission first, and only then our gradual promotion. To reach that future, *God requires our obedience before our understanding.*

GOD PROMOTES IN HIS PERFECT TIMING

As David obeyed, God continued opening new doors to his future. Killing Goliath gave him favor with Saul, and he was made a leader of Saul's army. This, in turn, earned him credibility before the people. Because David persevered, because he was faithful each step of the way, because he did not give up, in God's perfect timing he became king.

> *David was thirty years old when he became king, and he reigned forty years.*
>
> 2 SAMUEL 5:4

David endured many injustices, dangers, and hardships until God's image was so fused to David's soul that we still see it today in his story and his writings.

David embraced his place. Do you know the ultimate plans God had for him? Not only did David become the greatest king of Israel, not only did he pen some of the most eloquent and beloved words of Scripture, but he also was given the privilege of playing his part in the lineage of Jesus Christ. Paul's words about David, spoken generations later, reveal those astounding plans:

> *From this man's descendants God has brought to Israel the Savior Jesus, as he promised.*
>
> ACTS 13:23

You and I face a huge question: Do we trust God to do in his own timing what only he can do?

Do you trust him enough to believe he is at work in your present relationships? Do you trust him enough to persevere in your current responsibilities? Are you willing to remain faithful and patient in this season, in these circumstances, no matter what you must endure? Will you be diligent in cultivating your heart for God, in worshiping him, in abiding in his Word, in doing his work?

This is exactly what God is asking of you. This trust enables you to say:

"Yes, Lord, I will fight for the survival of this difficult marriage."

"Yes, I will remain honest through this bad financial situation."

"Yes, I will continue to serve in this ministry through every challenge."

"Yes, I will love my child selflessly, even when I am despised for it."

"Yes, I will take the high road and offer forgiveness in this broken relationship."

This is living in obedience before understanding. This kind of trust grows when you embrace your place.

GO WITH WHAT YOU <u>DO</u> KNOW

Where are you right now in embracing your place? Whether you are eighteen or eighty, you don't yet know the full story of what God plans to accomplish *through* you in this world. But you do know what he plans to accomplish *in* you. He plans to make you more and more like Jesus. In light of that truth, consider how freed up you can be by the principles we have just discussed in learning to embrace your place.

You now know that *God chooses the part you play in the body.* You no longer have to vie for a more prominent position or begrudge your current status. Instead, you can be watching for the character and experiences God is building into your life, enjoying your newfound confidence in God's perfect plan.

You now know that *God prepares those he calls.* So see your past and into your future through new eyes, recognizing all the ways God has intervened to prepare you for a life filled with meaning and purpose and love. You can ask God to help you see your present as preparation for how he will use you in the future, learning to trust and obey even before you understand. This enables you to be faithful in unwelcome circumstances and trials, even though they may hurt, because you can appreciate that God is at work in you.

You now understand that *God promotes in his perfect timing.* This understanding allows you to practice patience as God's will unfolds, even when his will seems slow. Your confidence will grow that he will promote you to the next level of service by steering you into your next exchange zone. This realization will enable you to be ready to release the baton you are carrying in order to accept the new baton he offers you.

Given these truths then, in trust and obedience, go with what you *do* know rather than fret over what you *don't* know. Love God. Obey him. Trust him. Serve him. Do the next right thing and joyfully thank him for what he is accomplishing inside of you.

Will you trust God enough to embrace your place? Then pray now.

God, I trust you. No matter what happens, I believe that you are at work for my eternal best and my part in your kingdom. Even when I can't see it or understand it, I believe it. I offer you my obedience no matter what I encounter. Do whatever it takes, Lord, to prepare me for the future you have in mind for me. Amen.

Rejoice! God is building his strength and character in you, growing your capacity to carry greater batons, one after another, into a future you have not yet imagined, across a finish line that, though still shrouded in fog, God describes in this way:

"I know the plans I have for you," declares the Lord, "plans to prosper you and not to harm you, plans to give you hope and a future."
JEREMIAH 29:11

CHAPTER 5

NEVER STAND STILL IN THE EXCHANGE ZONE

Kristen drew a steadying breath as she stepped into the prestigious Cecil B. Day Chapel of the Carter Center in Atlanta and took in the elegant surroundings. The raised hardwood stage with its dramatic three-story backdrop of windows bathed the auditorium in soft, filtered daylight. Everything about this room — the two tiers of cushioned chairs, the highly polished wood trim accenting the walls and stately columns, the whispered hush of perfect acoustics — created an aura of official dignity.

She found it hard to believe that she would soon step onto that stage to address more than three hundred people — professional educators, various law enforcement personnel, FBI agents, first responders, political and community leaders, and journalists. This conference, hosted by the Georgia Department of Education, had been called to discuss the impact of human trafficking on the students of Georgia and to explore how the schools and community could join the fight against it.[10]

Every one of these attendees and presenters is at least twice my age, Kristen thought. Only twenty-two years old, she tried not to feel intimidated. *Lord, every doubt and insecurity inside of me is screaming for me to run home,* Kristen prayed. *But I know that when you call, you qualify and equip. I am stepping out in obedience, knowing you have sent me here and promised to go with me.* She suddenly felt a calm pour over her and smiled at the memory of her A21 teammates gathered around her, praying for this day. She knew they were praying at this very moment. More confident in God's peace, she took her seat. One by one, various presenters took the stage to shed light on the extensive problem of child sex trafficking, emphasizing that it wasn't only an international problem but a local one as well. She heard the estimates that every single month, more than four hundred children, both internationals and locals, were trafficked in Georgia, being transported via freeways and airports and abducted or hawked as chattel everywhere from cities to migrant camps to business districts to the suburbs. She could tell by their reaction that this shocked many in the audience. But nothing she heard surprised her. She'd been researching the horrors of sex trafficking for six years, since she'd first heard of it as a teenager.

She checked the time on her muted cell phone, then stood and slipped up the aisle to await her cue to move onto the stage. When she stepped up to the podium, she felt a profound sense of astonishment that God was using her at such an event. Her earlier nervousness now prayed away, she scanned the illustrious group of leaders, humbled yet confident that God had chosen her to bring this vitally important message to this assembly.

Kristen started her talk by sharing the story of how she had joined the battle against sex trafficking when she first learned that girls like her were being sold into sex slavery around the world. She gave the testimonies of several women who'd been rescued through the work of The A21 Campaign and then presented the curriculum A21 was developing for use in high schools around the world. Her heart soared as she watched the audience taking copious notes and nodding with surprise as they listened. God was using her! These professionals were eager and hungry to hear of her personal experience and of the material that she, though young and inexperienced, had been entrusted by God to oversee. The audience offered an overwhelming response after her presentation. The attendees sought her out, eager to hear more. Excitedly, she distributed copies of the curriculum under development and gathered valuable feedback from many educators. Near the end of the conference, her jaw dropped when the Georgia Department of Education announced they would use the A21 curriculum in a pilot program in Georgia high schools. God had used her, of all people, to influence this assembly to bring lifesaving material into the lives of thousands!

THE VEIL IS LIFTED

That day, the veil was lifted just a bit for Kristen as she caught a glimpse of the sheer magnitude of the divine relay and her part in it. There were more lanes than she'd known. More runners than she'd imagined. God was on the move, and she'd not only been privy to how he was mobilizing people to attack the vicious evil of trafficking, but she could also see that God had orchestrated every step of her journey that led to this moment. He had propelled her into this lifesaving work to play a part in his plan.

As Kristen headed home from the conference, she thought back six years earlier to when another veil had been lifted — the day when, as a sixteen-year-old attending a Christian women's conference, she'd first heard the shocking reality of modern-day human trafficking. Little did she know then how that day would become a turning point that would launch her at top speed into the divine relay.

You mustn't miss what happened at that point, because Kristen is a perfect example of another principle in becoming an unstoppable runner in God's relay: *Never stand still in the exchange zone.* In fact, this is such an important principle I've learned in my relay that now I hand batons *only* to those who are already running. This chapter will show you why.

When Kristen heard of the need to help save young women from the horror of trafficking, she felt moved to take action, to do something, *anything,* to help. So this tenderhearted teen returned to her friends at Hudsonville High School in Michigan and shared not only the tragic news of human trafficking but also the A21 plans to open the first ever safe house in Greece. *She saw a need and set out to meet it. She dreamed big, dove in, and reached out to others to join her.* Her high school friends were so inspired by her passion that they went to work dreaming up ways to raise awareness and funds for the cause.

Under Kristen's leadership, they sponsored a walk-a-thon in their town, challenged local schools to a "change war" to see who could collect the most spare change for the cause, and organized a battle of the bands among students. Motivated by the students' passion, their school officials and church youth leaders joined in, offering to dye their hair pink or shave their heads if the kids hit their goals — which they did!

Yes, Kristen ran. She was off in Michigan running laps and passing batons before we'd ever heard her name. She wasn't sure what would work and what wouldn't, but she didn't let that stop her. She just kept trying new things and, in the process, she and her friends began raising a considerable amount of funds and even more awareness.

As she ran, she grew. She learned how to assemble a team, how to cast vision, how to find her way around challenges and learn from mistakes as well as from success, and in the process she was learning how to be a strong, unstoppable runner.

During that time, Kristen connected by email with Annie, one of the original A21 team who'd helped launch our ministry.

A perceptive leader, Annie encouraged Kristen in her efforts and reported them back to the rest of our team. We were overjoyed that a sixteen-year-old had taken it upon herself to start running in the race to abolish this evil. To our amazement, this little band of high school friends collected $32,000 and sent it to us to help get the rescue house in Greece off the ground. Can you believe that?

ON-THE-JOB TRAINING

Because Kristen chose to run in the exchange zone rather than stand still, Annie and I saw Kristen in the race. So when we had a baton to pass along, we ran into Kristen's exchange zone and offered her the baton of an internship with A21 as she neared high school graduation. We'd been so impressed with her initiative and leadership, we invited her to come to Australia and join our team in building up our student initiatives. Given her on-the-job training, who could be better qualified?

However, Kristen had also been offered a full-ride college scholarship. She had a choice to make. "I knew that I could take either path and God would still have me involved in his kingdom work," Kristen explained. "Either way, I would be blessed and able to touch people's lives and make a difference. But I felt an urge, a call, to join The A21 Campaign. Deep down I knew that by working for A21, it would be more about who I was becoming than what I was going to accomplish."

She had that right! How is that for moving into the future God has for you? Kristen had two good lanes to choose from, but knew that to run the race she was made for, she had to choose one and turn away from the other. She chose the one that she believed would most stretch her spiritual life.

Kristen joined our team, and we had the privilege of watching her grow. She ran well. She was faithful with every baton given to her, even batons such as managing the back end of our website for a season because we didn't have anyone else at the time. Despite her inexperience and lack of a "calling" to website work, Kristen embraced her place. She accepted every responsibility she was given, and, as a result, she developed skills she would never have learned if she had refused to be stretched. In fact, she didn't just accept each responsibility — she owned it, and in owning it, she demonstrated one of the qualities that made her so unstoppable: the willingness to tackle the tasks at hand, even those she didn't necessarily want to do. The result? Each new task strengthened her and increased her capacity, flexibility, and endurance. If you stop running because you don't like a particular aspect of your race, you will miss out on the growth that comes from being stretched beyond your comfort zone.

Kristen ran so well and increased her personal capacity so much that, three years later, we asked her to oversee the curriculum project we hoped would be used in high schools around the globe to raise awareness, prevent new victims, and stimulate new solutions to the problem. Though Kristen was not a trained educator, though she was without a college degree, though she'd never written curriculum before, *she had been running in the lane of student initiatives and growing in her ability.* We'd seen how God had grown her gifts in leadership, servanthood, and spiritual insight.

Kristen accepted the baton of directing curriculum development, and again she excelled. That led me to choose her to represent A21 at the conference in Georgia that opened this chapter, and today, thanks to Kristen's work, God is multiplying those efforts many thousand-fold in the US alone and who knows how much globally. That day when she stood on the conference stage, she tossed out batons right and left. Many people caught those batons, and once again we see how God's unstoppable divine relay stretches across time and distance, carrying the work of God's kingdom into countless lives.

When Kristen returned home to our office in California after her presentation in Georgia, I was so proud of her I thought I would burst. She'd run well, and I knew the baton our team had handed her — to represent us at this conference — had been placed in the hand of the right runner for the job.

Today in Kristen's work at A21, she manages a team of highly qualified educators twice her age who are scattered around the world, crafting and refining the curriculum. Because she and A21 value education and professionalism, she is also a university student, learning all she can to excel even more at the work she's been called to do. She is trustworthy, accountable, and persistent, yet she remains humble, ever aware that God's on-the-run training built the skills she would need to carry each subsequent baton.

"I knew that from a human perspective, I was not qualified to be on that stage," Kristen said. "I did not have the life experience, knowledge, charisma, or education level of anyone else who spoke that day. But I do have the Holy Spirit in me who empowers me by his grace and power. I learned that day in a profound way that God is really the only qualifier we need." It is one thing to be able to quote a Scripture and an entirely different thing to live it out. In that assembly Kristen felt the reality of this Scripture verse:

> *He said to me, "My grace is sufficient for you, for my power is made perfect in weakness." Therefore I will boast all the more gladly about my weaknesses, so that Christ's power may rest on me.*
>
> 2 CORINTHIANS 12:9

The Christian life is always, always on-the-job training.

WE ARE HIS HANDIWORK

In the divine relay, there is no place for idleness or procrastination. The race is on! When you are running with your hand reaching back, palm open, ready and waiting, the baton finds you. God will place it in your open hand. As long as you keep running, God is equipping you to do the work at hand, all the while preparing you in ways you've never imagined to do the next work he will call you to do. God is always at work leading you, training you, and shaping your heart and passions.

But such growth is dependent on never growing stagnant — never standing still in the exchange zone. Just as you cannot steer a ship that isn't moving, batons cannot pass between those who are not running. We must keep moving!

Remember the relay in the Olympic races? The starter breaks away from the starting line. Runner number two is in the exchange zone and begins to run, then accelerates, then reaches back and runs flat-out, eyes fixed forward, never back, and keeps running until that baton is slapped into his or her hand. What would happen if the second runner were standing still? This is a *race*, not a leisurely stroll or a meandering walk. A race. If the person in the exchange zone were standing still, both runners potentially could be knocked over and the race would be lost! There is no way for the team to get that baton across the finish line first unless every runner is already running, arm reaching back and ready.

How did those runners win their places on the team? By running, running, and running some more. Practice increased their strength and improved their speed. Coaching as they ran honed their skills, enhanced their techniques, and pushed them to excel.

God not only powerfully uses people who are runners — "just do something" kinds of people — he trains them by keeping a steady supply of new batons flowing into their lives and thereby grows their capacity to have an impact on this world. This is what happens when we do God's work. *We develop to the level of where we need to go. As we move and serve and run for God, we, like Kristen, grow in experience, strength, courage, confidence, tenacity, and endurance.*

Today Kristen laughs at the memory of her first response when I asked her to make that presentation.

"I freaked out when Chris first asked me to be the one to go present in Georgia," Kristen said. "Why me? I'd expected her to go. She'd have blown the roof off the place! I was nervous and instantly had doubts and thoughts of insecurity. But as I prayed about it, I realized it was clearly a God thing. God had placed me there for a reason. I had to choose to step out in obedience and rely on his promises to meet me there."

Kristen sees from her experience that as long as we run with our eyes fixed on Jesus, we learn, we grow, we stretch, and we become better runners than ever before. God is never merely accomplishing temporal results. God is always working on us and in us for our eternal good and his glory.

Do you see what God does when we don't stop but keep moving? God gladly steers a moving ship. The same will be true for you. Don't come to a standstill when you hit daunting challenges or new territory. Don't wait to serve, hoping to grow qualified before you take the next step. Be faithful in running, even if you, like Kristen, find yourself running into intimidating situations. Keep running, confident that God will train you as you run. Pray and reach for the next baton — and watch how God shapes you into an unstoppable runner as he coaches and challenges you on the run.

WHAT KIND OF GOD?

Kristen exemplifies the stages we've covered in these first five chapters. As a sixteen-year-old believer, she'd already committed herself to be a runner in God's divine relay and attended a conference to help her grow in her ability to run. Seeing an evil in this broken world, she didn't consider the impossibility of stopping human trafficking; instead, she believed God could use her new knowledge of that evil as a starting point for her own run.

Believing that God had qualified her to do her part, even if she didn't yet know how, she offered herself to him, and he immediately multiplied her efforts. As she embraced the place where God had her — her local high school and youth group — she carried her passion for God's race to her friends and community. She didn't sit there idle, waiting for someone to tell her what she could do or how. She simply ran and, in doing so, she grew in her abilities, her skills, and her confidence, not only boldly handing off batons to others who joined the race because of her, but also finding new batons placed in her open, outstretched hand.

Kristen has it right when she says, "I don't have to be the most qualified person in the race. I just need to show up, do the part that I'm being asked to play, and then I begin to discover that I am *benefiting* from it. As I'm pouring out my efforts for God, God is pouring his life into me."

What kind of God sends a twenty-two-year-old girl with no college degree into a Department of Education conference of professionals to inspire them to adopt a curriculum that she is overseeing?

The same God who sends a murderer to lead his people out of slavery (Moses), a shepherd boy to kill a giant (David), a virgin to bear a savior (Mary), a child to give his meager lunch (the uncounted boy), a common fisherman to lead his church (Peter), an unqualified Aussie to rescue sex slaves (me), and *you* to do his work on this earth.

Yes, you are in the very same lineup as all the other champions of the faith. God's unstoppable relay is filled with willing runners who have chosen to not stand still but to run from exchange zone to exchange zone, always receiving his on-the-job training for the work he has planned for us to do.

For we are God's handiwork, created in Christ Jesus to do good works, which God prepared in advance for us to do.

EPHESIANS 2:10

CHAPTER 6

THE MYSTERY REVEALED

I could hardly breathe for the wonder of it all.

It was a Sunday evening in January 1989 when I first stepped into what looked to me like a warehouse rather than a church. I took my seat on a folding chair among several hundred people, not sure what to expect from a church so different in appearance from the traditional sanctuary I'd attended as a child. The next thing I knew, I was surrounded by the joyful sound of voices lifted in wholehearted praise. I saw faces and arms lifted to heaven; I heard the Word of God proclaimed; I heard heartfelt prayers taken to the throne of God. I was overwhelmed with an experience I had no words to describe but now know as a worship service. Whatever this was, I wanted more, and I somehow knew I'd found what I did not even know I was looking for — a church family. A spiritual home.

An announcement was made that people were needed to help set up chairs one night that week, and I couldn't wait to volunteer.

From then on, every time those church doors were open, I was there. If the church needed volunteers to scrub floors, wash windows, clean out closets, rearrange furniture, organize the storage room, you name it, I was there.

The church was young and vibrant and graciously reached out and welcomed everyone to join in and become a part of what was happening. I got the message immediately. "Hey, if you're willing, have a go at it! Join in. Take part." You didn't have to get your life all cleaned up before you could serve. You didn't have to wait twenty years or pass a theology test to earn your place. Every service, every event, cried out to me with open arms of acceptance that seemed to say, "Come just as you are and join us in being transformed by God from the inside out." I got involved in a heartbeat. I was all in and loving it.

I started a Bible-reading plan. I started to journal. I joined a small group. For the first time in my life, I developed a daily intimate relationship with the Holy Spirit of God. God's Spirit began convicting me of sin and prompting me to burn some destructive bridges to my past.

Driven by an insatiable appetite for God's truth, I bought the pastors' teaching tapes and listened to the week's sermons multiple times each week. Everything about the way I saw God, the world, and myself was radically changing because I was in the Word every day. I became aware, for the first time, of the work of the Holy Spirit in me to open my eyes to the power and truth of his Word.

One day I read this verse in Isaiah:

> Then I heard the voice of the Lord saying, "Whom shall I send? And who will go for us?" And I said, "Here am I. Send me!"
>
> ISAIAH 6:8

A deep passion stirred the core of my being. A powerful desire swept over me to go all over the world telling others of this Jesus who was radically transforming my life. I didn't have a clue as to how I would do that or what it would look like. I only knew I yearned to share with the world the deep love I was experiencing.

There was a mystery at work in me. I did not know how this mystery was happening. I did not yet have the vocabulary to explain it. But I knew something mysterious, something glorious and wonderful, was happening inside of me.

Paul, in his letter to the Colossians, explains it beautifully.

> *We continually ask God to fill you with the knowledge of his will through all the wisdom and understanding that the Spirit gives, so that you may live a life worthy of the Lord and please him in every way: bearing fruit in every good work, growing in the knowledge of God.*
>
> COLOSSIANS 1:9 – 10

This is precisely what I was experiencing — the knowledge of God's will was infiltrating my life and I was beginning to "bear fruit," meaning that I was making a difference in the lives of others through the good work God was entrusting to my care. The Spirit of God was giving me wisdom and understanding beyond my own limited perspective as my knowledge of God — his heart, his purposes, his ways — was growing. Paul goes on a few verses later to reveal that he has been commissioned by God to reveal *a mystery.*

> *God gave me [the commission] to present to you the word of God in its fullness — the mystery that has been kept hidden for ages and generations, but is now disclosed to the Lord's people. To them God has chosen to make known among the Gentiles the glorious riches of this mystery.*
>
> COLOSSIANS 1:25 – 27

What a buildup he is giving this mystery. Finally, he reveals it:

This mystery, which is Christ in you, *the hope of glory.*

COLOSSIANS 1:27, EMPHASIS ADDED

The something wonderful that I'd been experiencing was Christ in me.

THE MYSTERY AT WORK

Eleven months flew by. In that time, under sound teaching, and feeding on God's Word, I began to understand that all these changes I'd been experiencing were *Christ in me* reshaping my heart. During this time, I had my "embrace your place" lesson with Jeremy in the youth center, when *Christ in me* prompted me to serve in humility and tangibly demonstrate God's love through good works. I was now running my part in God's divine relay, and as I ran, *Christ in me* was growing in the knowledge of God.

One November day, on a Tuesday, I went to the church in response to an announcement that help was needed to clean up a storeroom. I walked in to discover I was the only one who'd turned up to clean that day. I enjoy bringing order out of chaos (Nick will tell you I can be a bit obsessive about needing everything in its proper place) and finished the job quickly.

As I walked out of the storeroom, the assistant youth pastor, John, was standing at the top of the stairs, and he said, "You're Christine Caryofyllis, aren't you?" (My maiden name. I told you I was Greek.)

My heart pounded. In those eleven months, I'd hardly spoken a word to any leader in the church. I'd felt like a kid just grateful to watch them from a distance and do the physical work that needed doing.

"Um, yeah" was the most profound response I could muster.

"I've noticed you a lot. You're always around."

I beamed, shocked to learn I'd been noticed. "Yeah. I just love it here."

"You've got a degree in psychology, don't you?"

I didn't. I had just done two years of introductory psychology and was majoring in English and economic history, so I filled him in, then said, "I can read Golden Books and count to ten. That's about it."

He smiled. "Well, look, we've just got a government grant to start a youth center. I'm going on a missions trip with our senior pastor for a few weeks, and when I come back, I'd love you to have researched it and just find us somewhere to start the youth center."

I stood there slack-jawed, a dumbfounded look on my face, and stared at him.

And then a remarkable thing happened. He reached to his belt, unclipped his pager (another gadget invented before cell phones in prehistoric times, along with camera film), and, from the top of the stairs, he tossed it to me.

Instinctively my hands went up and I caught it. It looked like an ordinary pager. But do you know what it really was?

It was a baton.

I hadn't come looking that day for a major assignment from the pastor. At that point in my spiritual understanding, I wouldn't have dreamed I was even worthy of one. I thought I'd just shown up to clean the church. But God had positioned me in that place at that time. He'd led me to my lane at Hillsong Church, where I'd been running, faithfully serving behind the scenes; and finally, when he knew I was ready, he'd run me, unaware, straight into the exchange zone and tossed me a pager with a job to do.

I gulped. I heard myself accept the assignment, and I left the building wondering how someone as unqualified as I could have agreed to such a thing. What did I know of government grants or running a youth center? I'd never even attended a youth ministry event until five months before, and I was filled with only questions, not answers. I knew nothing about the hows or whys or whats of a Christian youth center. I didn't even know my way around the Bible yet! Why had I agreed? Why hadn't I explained to him that I knew absolutely nothing?

I saw only my limitations. This frightened me. But thanks to the heart changes growing inside me, I didn't respond as I would have in the past. The old Christine would have quit before she started out of the fear of failure and not being good enough. But the new Christine was willing, in spite of her fear, to step out in faith. I was about to discover that it is only when we hit the limits of our own strength and resources that we learn to rely not on our own sufficiency, but on the all-sufficiency of Christ *in* us.

DISCOVERING THE POWER OF CHRIST IN ME

The next six weeks, I was a woman with a mission. Scared or not, I was so excited to be entrusted by Pastor John with my new responsibility, I decided to put into practice what I'd been reading in God's Word and hearing preached. I decided to step out in faith and try. Since I didn't have a clue how to research the opening of a youth center, my daily prayer and devotional time took on a new focus: *Dear God, please show me what to do.*

This was a turning point for me. The old Christine would have relied on her own strengths and resources. But that old Christine was shrinking away as *Christ in me* was growing larger. I was now willing to admit my weakness and ask God and others for help without fear of looking foolish. I was now able to pray and believe that God would answer. I was daring to take one step of faith, ready and eager for it to lead to another. You guessed it — I was running, openhanded, ready for God's on-the-job training. And God had just the right lesson ready for me to learn: *Rely on God's power, not your own.* This is another principle we must grasp if we are to be unstoppable in our race.

After seeking God's guidance, I looked for every community-based youth center within a twenty-mile radius and visited all of them. I asked every question I could think of about what they were doing, why, and how. I took notes and discovered that we just had to identify the practical needs of youth in our local community and then meet them. Next, I learned I had to get the word out that we were there to serve our community.

God, you and I know I haven't got the slightest idea what I'm doing, I'd pray each morning, *so please give me your favor.* Then I'd set up meetings with Rotary clubs and local business leaders and the police department, and I'd walk in and introduce myself with, "Hi, I'm Christine from the Hills District Youth Service." I asked questions like, "What are the needs? How can we serve you? What are the biggest problems for young people in this community?"

I discovered there was no shortage of needs, just a shortage of resources and people to meet them. As I began to pray for God to use us to meet those needs, I realized we didn't have the resources to accomplish that enormous task. It was another revelation from Christ at work in me: *Rely on God's resources, not your own.*

Young people needed a safe place to drop in and hang out, to meet up with friends where they'd be drawn by the music they loved and feel comfortable and welcomed. They needed alternatives to illegal graffiti to express their creativity. Migrant young people needed classes in English as a second language so they could function in school and get jobs. Students needed drug education, abstinence training, self-esteem coaching, and help in coping with bullying and abuse. There were young people in detention centers who needed visitors and positive influences. There were young people in trouble who needed someone they could trust. Where would we get the people to do these things? Where would we get the money for supplies? Who would provide such training? Where would we get the building for all this to take place?

The more I learned, the more I asked God to use us to meet those needs, and the more excited I became about the difference we could make in these young people's lives.

God used my naïveté and wide-eyed question asking, and my inexperience with the financial constraints of such undertakings, to open doors of communication that I didn't know were seldom open between the culture and the church at the time. It's amazing how people will let you in if you are willing to serve. Businesses started offering supplies, paint, furniture, and even tradesmen to help us create our youth center. I walked into meetings relying on God and looking only for information, and walked out with new friends who wanted to help us succeed.

In my Bible reading, I was discovering verses like James 4:2:

You do not have because you do not ask God.

I'd been experiencing a church of such vibrant faith that it did not occur to me that the verse might not mean what it said. So I asked God for his provision for our youth center. I read, "The Lord is with you," so I just assumed that he was with me, and my growing confidence in him emboldened me as I went into each of my meetings. People started volunteering their help and services, which inspired more people to do the same, because they were all eager to see young people helped and at-risk young people guided in the right direction. They all loved the idea of a youth center designed for the specific needs of our community. I was seeing God answer prayers right before my eyes.

What was happening? *Christ in me* was taking hold of my thinking and expanding his influence in my heart.

Every need, every idea, every potential resource went into the report I was preparing for Pastor John. From what I'd researched so far and the resources we'd been offered, I figured we could open a drop-in center to get started. What a contrast to my old ways, when I wouldn't have dared to dream of beginning a new venture unless I'd been personally able, under my own power, to map out every detail of how to achieve every objective. Seeing God provide such resources and so many people willing to help, I was catching on to the way he worked. I didn't need to know what these programs would look like or how they'd be run. I didn't have to figure it all out in advance. Clearly, God had a plan in place, and he was unfolding it before me. I was learning to put yet another principle to work: *Rely on God's ways and not your own.*

Did I mention that we were also given a building? That's right. We asked and were given the old police station as the new home of the Hills District Youth Service. It was as if, from day one, God wanted me to understand and believe that what he expected from me was a willing heart to place all that I had in his hands, expecting that he would provide the rest. And he did!

God was demonstrating to me what happens when we step out and accept his baton. I showed up to worship and accepted an invitation to clean out a storeroom. Out of the cleaning came the pager. Out of the pager came the ability to set up meetings with the community and the police department. Out of that came a flourishing youth center and a job as its associate director, then director. And out of that came meetings with the prime minister of Australia, because the youth center grew in influence. Relying on God's power, his resources, and his ways, we provided services for every one of those needs I listed earlier, and when we opened the doors of that youth center, we were given the privilege of opening young hearts to the power and person of Jesus Christ.

THE TRUE WORK OF THE BATON

One day, as we were working on our plans, Pastor John said, "Chris, we've got to find a way to bring you on staff." There was nothing in the grant that could be applied to staffing, but there was a sixty-dollar-per-week provision for a janitor.

He looked me straight in the eyes and asked, "Would you be

willing to quit your job and accept a sixty-dollar-per-week stipend to come on full time as an associate director of the youth center?" It was an absurd idea. I had completed my university degree and had just been offered a five-figure contract working for a shipping company, which was great money for a new graduate. But I quickly pushed that aside.

"Yes, I'll do it!" I answered from the depths of my heart.

I'd been running, baton in hand. *Christ in me* had taken hold and was expanding my faith and knowledge of God. I knew deep in my spirit that I was gaining something in this work that was far more than could be measured in dollars. I was growing richer in my soul.

As *Christ in me* had been expanding to fill me more and more, I was experiencing a transformation — my faith was growing larger. My understanding of God and his power was expanding exponentially. And this is when it dawned on me.

I'd thought the goal of the race was earning God's favor.

I'd thought the baton was good works.

I'd thought the race was about me trying hard enough to do enough good works for God, to carry enough good works across the finish line, that I'd earn his love.

I'd thought the exchange zone was me coming back to God for the next job to do, and then the next, because no matter what good works I'd already done, they were never enough, so I needed to do the next good work, hoping it would bring me closer to earning God's favor.

But that wasn't it at all!

Since Pastor John had tossed me that pager — that baton — the carrying of that baton had been transforming me. As I'd seen God provide answers to prayer, resources beyond expectation, people to help, and experts to advise, I'd learned to rely on God's power, God's resources, and God's ways rather than my own. My small image of God had been overcome with how huge and mighty and inexplicably vast he truly is. My faith in him had grown. My trust in him had expanded. My love for him had deepened. Do you understand?

- The goal of the race *is not* to earn God's favor. *The goal is to become more like Christ.*
- The baton *is not* doing good works. *The baton is Christ at work in me and through me to the world.*
- Receiving the baton is not simply accepting a task to do for God. *Receiving the baton is inviting God to work in me and through me.*
- The race *is not* my lifelong efforts of doing good works to earn God's love. *The race is the process of becoming like the one I'm running toward, Jesus Christ.*
- The exchange zone is not where I come for more works to do. *The exchange zone is the transformation zone. It is where I show up, ready and willing, for the next baton — the next work of God in me and through me to the world SO THAT my transformation to Christlikeness continues.*

You must understand this if you plan to be unstoppable in your race! Otherwise, you risk building your Christian life on only half the gospel and not the whole. You see, we do not become unstoppable because our talents are so great or our good works are so impressive. *Christ in us* is unstoppable! Two things are at work as Christ in us expands:

- One: Christ in us transforms us to be like him. In theological terms, this is called sanctification. Remember from the Colossians verse earlier to *"live a life worthy of the Lord, ... growing in the knowledge of God."*
- Two: Christ in us transforms the world through us. Just as he did while he physically walked this earth, Christ in us

reaches out to broken people in a broken world. Through us he feeds the hungry, heals the sick, befriends the lonely, gives hope to the hopeless, and saves the lost. He loves this world through meeting needs. This is what works are about.

When we carry the baton, *both* things are accomplished! In my encounter with Jeremy, for instance, "works" were done. As I was providing a safe place for him to drop in and have a meal and be shown care, respect, and love, I myself was being transformed to be more like Christ in that my heart was changed to love Jeremy as God loved him. Just as in the Hills District Youth Service, works were done in that young people were helped, cared for, taught, and equipped for life, so too transformation occurred in the workers as Christlikeness grew in us through our serving these young people. Just as in A21, works are done in that people are rescued from slavery and fed and clothed and healed and restored, so too transformation occurs as bitterness is released, forgiveness is granted, faith is grown, and God is revealed.

And even more, the interplay of works and transformation to Christlikeness becomes an unstoppable, self-perpetuating cycle. The more we become like Christ, the more we love God, so the more we love people and the more works we want to do to help them. This forces us to rely on God's power, God's resources, and God's ways, and as we do, our old self shrinks away and Christ in us expands and we become even more like Christ.

Do you see why I want to spend my life eagerly running into the exchange zone for baton after baton after baton? I never want to stop! And once you experience the power of God working in and through you, I believe you won't want to stop either! Every baton brings us closer to Christlikeness. Every baton displays his love and power to the world. As we carry it, it changes us, which spurs us to hand it off to others so they too can be changed. As long as we run, Christ in us is at work. And he never stops working in us. Of this, we can be confident!

> *Being confident of this, that he who began a good work in you will carry it on to completion until the day of Christ Jesus.*
>
> PHILIPPIANS 1:6

BECOMING WHOM YOU'RE RUNNING TOWARD

The Bible is full of ordinary people whom God called to his divine relay. Which of them, in their power, their resources, or their ways had what was required to do what God called them to do? Not one.

Moses was told to lead his people from slavery, then was caught between Pharaoh's chariots and the Red Sea. Joshua was told to conquer the walled city of Jericho armed with nothing more than trumpets. Gideon was told to defeat the massive Midianite army after the Lord purposefully shrank his army from 32,000 men to only 300 armed with nothing more than trumpets, torches, and empty jars. Peter was beckoned by Jesus to get out of the boat and walk on water.[11]

Are you catching the theme here? Just like these people, when we learn to focus on who God is rather than on what we are not, we see that it is God who is working in us to do the very thing he has purposed to do in our lives. As we learn to run the race, accept his batons, and submit to his training, God's work in and through us is always growing and increasing. Christ in us becomes an unstoppable force in our lives and is spilled out into the lives of others.

Carrying the baton in our race is never about what *we* can accomplish *for* God. If he wanted, God could accomplish everything on his own without us, just as he created the heavens and the earth. He could have slain Pharaoh's army and horses in midstep and melted the chariots in the blink of an eye. He could have brought the walls of Jericho down as Joshua and his men were sleeping. He could have turned the massive Midianite army to stone before Gideon's men blew a trumpet. He could have transformed the wild waves beneath Peter's feet to solid rock. God's goal in each of those cases was to do far more than accomplish a task — it was to build the faith of his people. He wanted them to grow in their experience of him. He wanted his people to taste his power and be transformed by his might.

As you continue in your race, refuse to focus on what you are not, what you cannot do, and what you do not know. Rely on God's power. Rely on God's resources. Rely on God's ways. Focus on who Christ is in you. This is fixing your eyes on Jesus!

As you carry your baton, Christ's unstoppable power is expanding in you. His impact on your world is going to increase. His transformation in you is going to increase. Once you've grasped this mystery — Christ in you — you will transform the world through acts of love *and* you will be continually transformed on the inside to become more like him.

I pray that out of his glorious riches he may strengthen you with power through his Spirit in your inner being, so that Christ may dwell in your hearts through faith. And I pray that you, being rooted and established in love, may have power, together with all the Lord's holy people, to grasp how wide and long and high and deep is the love of Christ, and to know this love that surpasses knowledge — that you may be filled to the measure of all the fullness of God.

Now to him who is able to do immeasurably more than all we ask or imagine, according to his power that is at work within us, to him be glory in the church and in Christ Jesus throughout all generations, for ever and ever! Amen.

EPHESIANS 3:16–21

CHAPTER 7

THROW IT OFF

"When you get to Greece, you will do whatever your cousin tells you to do," the witch doctor said.

And Favour, kneeling before the witch doctor, repeated, "When I get to Greece, I will do whatever my cousin tells me to do."

"You will not speak to strangers."

"I will not speak to strangers."

"You will not tell anyone who took you to Greece."

"I will not tell anyone who took me to Greece."

"And if you do, you will die or go mad."

Shocked, Favour gasped. *Those* words she could not bring herself to repeat.

And why was she having to repeat *any* words a witch doctor prompted her to say?

"I was brought up by my dad and stepmother in Nigeria," Favour said, "and they treated me very badly. They beat me all the time." Favour's mother had deserted the family when Favour was only two years old. "I was miserable. When I was sixteen, my dad told me to leave his house and find somewhere else to stay."

Favour lived the next two years with a married couple and their five children in a small apartment, working as a housemaid — and fending off the husband's sexual harassment and advances. When she was eighteen, her cousin invited her to come to Greece. "I accepted because I needed money to study to become a nurse. I have a passion to care for people and give them hope. I was excited!"

But then the cousin told her that before she left Nigeria, she would need to see a witch doctor. "I was so scared! When he asked me to say that I would die or go mad if I broke my oath, I refused. But then they told me that if I did not say the words, I would not leave the witch doctor's house alive, and I believed them. I had heard bad stories about witch doctors, about how they kill people and have the power to make someone go mad. So I repeated his words — I said the oath. And then he made me say that if I even *told* anyone about the oath, I would die. I believed that it was true."

HELD CAPTIVE BY THE ENEMY

In my years in ministry, I've been honored to witness God's power at work in the lives of many women, including former trafficking victims. Favour is one of those women. With a story that begins so shrouded in the darkness and deceit of the enemy, it's always astounding to see God's light pierce such darkness and God's truth overcome such deceit. Yet time and again in the divine relay, we are given front-row tickets to the miracle of God setting the captives free. Favour's is such a story.

The events of Favour's life bring into sharp focus the unavoidable reality that we have an enemy in this race. This enemy prowls about like a lion, seeking whom he may devour. If we run our race well, he has so much to lose! He's not an enemy to be taken lightly.

As we progress in our run, running from exchange zone to exchange zone — receiving, releasing, multiplying, and growing —

the enemy sees us faithfully and consistently following this God-ordained pattern, and he knows his territory is threatened. He will plot and scheme to thwart us in our run, to slow us down, to stop us in our tracks. For this reason we must ensure that we do not carry any additional weight into the race that the enemy could use as a weapon against us. The writer to the Hebrews encourages us accordingly:

> *Let us throw off everything that hinders and the sin that so easily entangles. And let us run with perseverance the race marked out for us.*
>
> HEBREWS 12:1

Favour's story is one of my favorites, not only because we see her move from the captivity of the enemy's deceit to a life of freedom but also because in her example we can all find the courage to throw off whatever hinders us in our own race.

FREEDOM FOR FAVOUR

Despite the frightening oath that Favour was forced to take before her cousin would bring her to Greece to live in her home, Favour was excited to go. After all, her cousin had been like a sister to her before moving to Greece. But soon after Favour arrived, she had her first disturbing shock: Her cousin had another woman physically beat Favour — for no apparent reason at all. After the beating, her cousin revealed what the promised job was to be: Favour would work as a prostitute. "I told her I could not do it. I could not sleep with men. But she told me that this was the only way to pay her back the money she used to bring me to Greece — 60,000 euros.

"I had no choice. I had taken an oath that whatever she told me to do, I would do. I was terrified! I saw no way out. I didn't know anyone and didn't want to die from breaking the oath. And I knew that if I didn't do what she wanted, she would beat me.

"Every day was like living in hell. Sometimes I had to service forty or fifty men a day. There were times when I wanted to commit suicide. When I got home, my cousin would take all the money from me. 'Remember the oath,' she would say, 'or you will go mad and die.'"

Favour survived two years of this — two years of praying that God would get her out of her living hell — until one day, at the medical clinic where the prostitutes were required by Greek law to report to be checked for diseases, a woman who had been sitting in the waiting room approached her. It was Kalli, part of the staff at our A21 shelter in Greece. You met Kalli in chapter 2.

Favour asked Kalli where she was from. When Kalli told her that she was from South Africa, Favour said quietly, "Speak English, then — the madam doesn't understand it." The madam from the brothel always accompanied the girls to the clinic, so she wasn't far away.

The two women spoke in English, and every now and then one of them would say something silly, and they would laugh as if they were just chatting. But actually, Kalli was asking Favour for her story, and when she found that Favour was a sex slave, Kalli asked why she didn't go to the police. "They told me that if I go to the police," Favour said, "they will tell their associates in Nigeria, who will kill my family."

The two women began to meet secretly before or after Favour's shift at the brothel. Favour was from the Christian part of Nigeria (there is a Christian part and a Muslim part), but she didn't know much about the faith. "Kalli spoke to me about Jesus for four months," Favour said. "Finally, I desired to accept Jesus because I believed that he is the only one who can save me from the pain of the life I lived. So one day, when I got home from the brothel, I prayed by myself on my bedroom floor to accept Jesus."

Not long after that night, the police, after months of investigation, conducted a raid on Favour's cousin's home and arrested everyone living there — her cousin, her cousin's boyfriend, and Favour. They were taken to the police station, and Kalli privately met Favour there. "I was very scared in the beginning," Favour said. "I was afraid that if my cousin learned that I had been talking to Kalli, and that was why we had been arrested, I would be beaten or even killed, as most girls are who speak out or try to escape. But Kalli told me they would help me through it all."

Kalli brought Favour to the A21 safe house, where she met other girls who had been in the same situation. They gave her a room to sleep in and food to eat. Soon, Favour was experiencing love and care as she never had before in her life. She was witnessing the love of God through the love in action of the A21 staff.

When the date for the trial of her traffickers came up, Favour was so afraid of facing them again, particularly her cousin, that when she got to the courthouse, she was shaking. The trial lasted two days. Favour said, "When the lawyers called and told us that the traffickers had been sentenced to four years in jail, I jumped up and down for joy. A weight had been lifted off my shoulders. I could live again!"

That day, upon hearing of the traffickers' convictions, Favour realized that she belonged not to her sex traffickers but to Jesus. Now she wanted to live for him. But there was more to becoming free, she discovered, than escaping the brothel. She'd suffered all her life — first abandoned as a child, then harassed by her employer, then forced into hopeless degradation as a sex slave. Favour recognized the anger, bitterness, and emotional scars she carried. She'd spent years contending with nightmares and fears, shame and guilt, feelings of worthlessness and hopelessness.

She came to realize that she had to shed those hindrances that kept her entangled in the emotions and attitudes of her old life.

And a huge part of that was learning to forgive. Favour's lesson in forgiveness didn't come easily — or quickly.

"The ones I found it hardest to forgive were my father, because he drove me away from home; my stepmother, because she treated me badly; and my cousin, because she lied to me and made me sleep with men for money. Those things hurt me badly, and forgiving those three took me a very long time."

A very long time. Favour's simple words compress a lot of pain and struggle into a small space. For her, as for us all, forgiveness was ... complicated. In many ways, it was like recovering from a horror movie in which she'd played the lead. First came trauma therapy and the physical healing of the considerable damage to her body. Then came counseling to help her work through issues of trust, guilt, and shame — no small task for any victim of trafficking! But her issues preceded her servitude as a prostitute by many years. They extended to her earliest memories.

But the same God who is accessible to you healed Favour's heart over time. As she grew to know God better, as she immersed herself in his Word, as she experienced the tender care of her A21 friends, Favour invited God to become bigger in her life than the injustices she'd suffered, than the wounds inflicted upon her body and psyche, than the horror and pain of her past. And because she did, she was able to throw off those things that hindered her and step into the "exceedingly abundantly above" future (Ephesians 3:20 NKJV) that God had prepared for her before the foundations of the world.

That same hope exists for all of us.

In Favour's case, casting aside that baggage made it possible for her to follow God's leading into a dream she had long held: "Today I am in nursing school, living independently in a rented house. A21 is still helping me with my living and school expenses. God has used them to restore my life and to help make my dreams come true. The time I spent with them has changed my life. They taught me how to forgive, how to make friends, how to love and care for others. All of my life is new."

CHOICES

Like each of us, Favour faced a choice: She could have surrendered to the temptation to harbor the hate and resentment against those who made her life hellish for years. Who would have more right to do that than women like Favour who have been forced to live a life of degradation, brutality, and humiliation? But that was not the choice she made. If Favour, so young in her faith and so betrayed by life, can find the wherewithal to cast aside, to throw off, the entanglements that would hinder God's work in her life, consider the hope that you can do the same.

What are some of those things that hinder and entangle? Here are just a few examples:

- Unforgiveness
- Bitterness
- Shame
- Rejection
- Offense
- Lust
- Greed
- Envy
- Deceit
- Insecurity
- Fear
- Doubt
- Indifference
- Apathy
- False belief systems

Do any of those things sound familiar? Does it sound like I took that list right from your own life?

I didn't. I took it from mine.

If you read my story in *Undaunted*, you know that I was left in a hospital, unnamed and unwanted — that I was marginalized because of my ethnicity, gender, and socioeconomic background. I was also sexually abused as a child for many years. Men I trusted betrayed that trust and my innocence. The *Oxford Dictionary* defines "abuse" as using an object for a purpose other than that for which it was designed. For twelve years, I was used for a purpose for which I was never designed. Let me tell you, that messes with you big-time. But these things did not stop God from using me. In fact, his determination was unstoppable! He used me not in spite of my past but *because* of my past!

The reality is that nothing I say or do will change those things. The past is set and can't be changed. What happened, happened. But I *can* make choices today that will determine my future. And so can you. By putting God at the center of our lives, by dealing with the issues that hold us back, and by recognizing that the plans of God for our future are bigger than the pain and regret of our past, we are able to get up from wherever we are at this moment and move forward.

I am so grateful I reconciled my past in Christ and moved on to the future he has for me. This decision impacts not only me but also everyone around me, including the generations that come after.

Cleaning out and renovating our internal world requires an ongoing, focused commitment on our part. If I've made it sound as if throwing off these things was a one-time shot that, once accomplished, was never required again, let me correct that. We must learn and continually relearn to focus on *Christ in us* at work. It has taken me years of hard work and persistent prayer to throw off the pain and wounds of my past and grow through them. I've needed to repeatedly return to the throne of grace and seek God's strength to forgive and grow. The work of throwing off often takes time and diligent effort.

Does this stop us from running? Of course not! Do you remember the mystery? It is as we run our race and carry our batons that we receive God's on-the-job training in Christlikeness. We aren't required, under our own strength, to throw off what hinders *in order* to take our part in the race. Instead, we are invited to throw it all off *as we run* our race.

If we want to be unstoppable in our race, we need to constantly challenge ourselves to clean out the internal world of our heart and mind so that we have more room to contain more of the power of God within us. Remember, as Christ in us grows larger, our old selves grow smaller. Unloading all the baggage of old sins makes a lot of room for Christ in us to grow.

I don't know what your past is. I don't know what pains or sorrows or sins you carry. But I do know that God can turn all of it around and use your past to give someone else a future. That's what Jesus does. The divine relay is all about passing the baton from one life to another, from one generation to the next. This is what happens when we answer his call, when we hear him say, "Follow me," and respond in obedience.

FORGETTING WHAT IS BEHIND

We all have things we need to throw off. In fact, we need to regularly take inventory, because it's surprising how quickly the things we once threw off can come back and cling to us once again. So take a moment right now. Pause and ask yourself, "What do I need to throw off in order to run well?" The list could be endless. Perhaps you are carrying resentment or selfishness or pride that is hindering your witness at your job. What about unresolved anger that is hurting your relationships? Or a lack of confidence and a spirit of defeat that hinder your ability to make wise choices as you run your race? Or a lack of financial planning and discipline that hamper your ability to be generous with your resources, even though you would love to be? Or unresolved issues from the past that are harming your parenting skills? Does deep-rooted anger continue to resurface in your marriage, causing you to say things you later regret? Does insecurity about your abilities or looks cause you to be judgmental and critical of others?

Are you tethered to negative things such as destructive friends, favorite sins, unhealthy lifestyles, or negative habits? Are you too enamored with positive things such as financial gain, career success, or plentiful leisure time that hold you back from giving the time and energy to run the race God calls you to run? Whatever it is that holds you back, throw it off. Live free from your past mistakes, hurts, and misconceptions. "The old has gone, the new is here!" the apostle Paul said in 2 Corinthians 5:17. That applies to the refuse of your past — and to the hope for your future.

Old habits die hard. Breaking our comfortable, familiar patterns takes work. Hard work. But if we don't break from our past, we'll never run toward our new future.

Here is the simple truth: We cannot go where we are going without leaving where we have been. So ask yourself, "What must I leave behind in order to serve God with my whole life?" In the divine relay, God is looking for runners who, like Paul, will say:

Whatever were gains to me I now consider loss for the sake of Christ. What is more, I consider everything a loss because of the surpassing worth of knowing Christ Jesus my Lord, for whose sake I have lost all things. I consider them garbage, that I may gain Christ.

PHILIPPIANS 3:7 – 8

Imagine the freedom that will come when you are willing to lose that garbage for the surpassing greatness of becoming an unstoppable runner in the work God calls you to do! Anticipate the joy of moving forward into the future he has for you! Toss away the garbage from your past and eliminate any way to go back. Make a defining decision of unhindered commitment to Jesus Christ and his cause, and step out in faith.

Do you want God to do something new in your life? Then stop doing the same old thing.

Do you want God to change your circumstances? Then be willing to change your life.

One thing I do: Forgetting what is behind and straining toward what is ahead, I press on toward the goal to win the prize for which God has called me heavenward in Christ Jesus.

PHILIPPIANS 3:13 – 14

YOU CAN CHANGE THE FUTURE

Once you've thrown off what you should not be holding on to, you are free to grasp new batons. You cannot be grabbing new batons if you are clutching old weights. Your capacity to grab a new baton is determined by how wide you open your hands as you await what God has in store for you.

When you are living for the race, you'll be running that race all week long, all month long, all year long, and all life long, actively and passionately seeking where God is at work and joining him in that work. You'll be intentionally and purposefully carrying your baton into the building where you work, into your interactions with your neighbors, into your community, your school, your grocery store, your bank, even your own kitchen, always on the lookout for what God wants to accomplish through you in every circumstance.

Just consider the power of carrying your baton into those places rather than dragging along the ball and chain of hurts and resentments, sins and scars, and old priorities that are not God's priorities. You will feel lighter and run as a beacon of light for the Lord's glory rather than hibernating in a dark den surrounded by the weights of the past. Such freedom awaits you as you throw off those things that hinder you from becoming an unstoppable runner in God's divine relay.

Are you ready to put an end to all that holds you back, so you can run like the wind into your next exchange zone, chomping at the bit for your next baton? Then do so. Put an end to it. Endings, it turns out, are the perfect place for a new start.

I have often thought of the story of Joseph — beloved by his father but betrayed and sold into slavery by his jealous brothers, betrayed by others and thrown into prison but rescued by God and raised to a position of prominence and power. *"You intended to harm me,"* he later told his brothers when God enabled him to use that position of power to help his whole tribe, *"but God intended it for good to accomplish what is now being done, the saving of many lives"* (Genesis 50:20).

God promises that the plans he has for you are for good and not for evil, to give you a future and a hope. Why would you choose to live weighed down by the past when his promises are beckoning you into your future? Cut yourself free from all that hinders and cast it all away so you can experience the truth of Psalm 40:1 – 3:

> *I waited patiently for the Lord;*
>   *he turned to me and heard my cry.*
> *He lifted me out of the slimy pit,*
>   *out of the mud and mire;*
> *he set my feet on a rock*
>   *and gave me a firm place to stand.*
> *He put a new song in my mouth,*
>   *a hymn of praise to our God.*
> *Many will see and fear the Lord*
>   *and put their trust in him.*

CHAPTER 8

MASTER THE HANDOFF

"I have always known one thing," Annie said. "I want to change the world. Careful what you ask for, right?"

That's the voice of experience talking! Annie, a master of handing off batons to others in the race, is in fact changing the world, though not without cost. A few of Annie's handoffs required her to relinquish a ministry she treasured, move far away from the family she adored, and say good-bye to the country of her birth. But she'll be the first to tell you that the rewards far outweigh the cost, and she wouldn't trade her journey for the world.

Yet as you are about to discover, when you learn to master the handoff as Annie has, your race is not marred by sadness or regrets. It is filled with excitement, joy, and adventure. You don't have time to linger over the past because you are too busy running into the future. When God determines that it is time to hand off a baton, it is only because we have taken it as far as we can and he has something else for us to do. After all, we need to let go of one baton in order to take hold of another.

Annie is a remarkable woman of God who joined Nick and me

in the early days of our ministry. She has continually grabbed and released batons on this daring adventure we share. Before we had even officially started The A21 Campaign, it was Annie who led a research trip around the world from Australia and helped us build the infrastructure required to facilitate this work from the ground up. From day one, she began recruiting and raising up new runners every step of the way. Things were moving so fast that she had to train others on the run and then let them keep running with one area of responsibility so she could establish another.

Remember young Kristen in chapter 5? It was Annie who recommended that we offer her an internship and Annie who mentored her, as she has so many others. It is the handoff where Annie particularly excels: she inspires, leads, trains, and mentors as she hands off batons with great success. I sometimes suspect she needs an air traffic controller monitoring all the batons coming in for a landing, only to take off again from her capable hands.

Annie's capacity to receive and then hand off one baton after another has led her on an influential and unpredictable life journey over the years. Releasing the batons entrusted to your care — batons you've carried well and marveled over as you've experienced God's supernatural work in you and through you — often requires a willingness to say good-bye, to let go, to move from the known to the unknown. But the rewards can be breathtaking, because in the handoff, you are privileged to play a part in God's unfolding plan not only for you but also for others.

"Over the years," Annie said, "my work has gone from building teams face-to-face in Nick and Chris's living room to helping build teams around the world. It's been a crazy, wild ride that has me constantly learning and growing. Only God could have multiplied our early efforts into such a dynamic and unstoppable movement. He has mobilized ten offices in nine countries, from volunteers cleaning toilets, to lawyers winning convictions against traffickers, to shelter moms, counselors, life-skills coaches, drivers, researchers, and prayer warriors. He did it all one baton, one handoff at a time."

Annie has demonstrated time and again a bold willingness to release batons she loves for the sake of moving God's work forward in this world. When I first met her nearly twenty years ago, she'd recently relinquished a ministry she loved to follow God's call to move to Australia.

"I told everyone that I was going overseas for only *one* year," she said. "Then one year turned into two. And two turned into seven."

I remember when it was time for Annie to move back to America to help us open our new office in California. That's when she was hit with a surprise (and so was I!).

"The week before my move back to American soil, a friend revealed that he was drawn to me and had been for some time. Needless to say, I was caught off guard, but I didn't think I'd have to give him the 'I just don't feel the same way' speech because I thought the ocean would soon make it obvious that dating would not work. However, the distance didn't deter him. He kept texting, and eventually I found myself pulled into a long-distance relationship. I fought it. I really did, mostly because I knew that a relationship with him meant that one day it might lead me to move to another foreign land. If there was one thing I knew about him it was this: he was called to build the church in Greece. I had to know that I not only loved this man, but that our callings aligned. Choosing him meant handing off batons I loved to carry."

Annie was torn between two countries — Greece versus America — but she was loyal to only one kingdom, the kingdom of God. She was torn between two families — her beloved, close-knit biological family versus the family of God — but loyal to the one Father of both, almighty God. I watched and prayed for her as she contemplated what it would mean if she let go of her single life and the many batons she was carrying and were to accept the new baton of marriage on another continent.

Over the years, I've watched Annie wrestle with the choices God sets before her and have seen a mature leader emerge. What impresses me most about her baton decisions is that she is able to discern and follow her greatest priority, even when choosing which beloved baton to release. This decision was no different.

"It took me two years," Annie said, "to make the decision to move to Greece. Thankfully, I'd be able to work out of our A21 office there, yet I knew that relocating would mean having to release batons so very close to my heart. I loved training our interns in our US office and overseeing the many programs I'd developed. I loved living in my homeland, the USA. There were many tears when I left, but after trying to fight loving this Greek man and trying to find any loophole that would allow me to walk away in good conscience, I *knew* I had to make this move."

And so she did. She opened her heart, opened her hand, and received the baton of engagement. Simultaneously, she developed a handoff plan for the long list of beloved ministry batons she'd been carrying. She had new runners to train and transition plans to create, but she embraced this next phase of her race with anticipation of the adventure ahead. How would the new runners reshape and influence the work she had been doing? She didn't dread such change; she welcomed it, knowing that the future was in God's hands and the race was his. Each new runner had been qualified and prepared by our divine coach. The handoff had always been her goal — she loved nothing more than working herself out of a job so that others could grow as she had.

Annie offered God a heart of open expectation for the next leg of her own race. She had a new language to learn, a new culture to embrace, a new country to love. At thirty-four, Annie had never been a wife. Now she'd be the wife of a pastor. Would she also become a mother — a baton she'd never counted on? Only God knew.

"Today, I am living in Thessaloniki, Greece," she said, "thrilled to be married to the man God led to me and still handing off batons locally and globally. I have no idea what batons are yet to come my way, but I know this: I still want to change the world, to advance the kingdom. I've still got batons in my hand, and I'm going to keep running, watching for God's clues as to when to pass off each baton and so multiply his work into the lives of others."

You, like Annie, will be called on to hand off your baton to others. You are not only called to run, you must not only reach and grasp and carry, but you must also learn to release the baton to others because you are running in an *inter*dependent relay race, not an *independent* sprint. God's design for the relay, the body of Christ at work, is as brilliant as it is essential for living a vibrant and fruitful Christian life.

Embrace this design and live it out, and the power of your impact will multiply inside you and through you into the world.

But what happens if you run your race as a solo and not a relay and hold onto your favorite batons, never releasing them? Sadly, many do just that with disastrous consequences. Take a look at what, to me, is one of the saddest portions of Scripture. It is found in Judges 2. I believe it offers a crucial warning for our time and place in church history.

A GENERATION WHO DID NOT KNOW GOD

Joshua was the man God chose to lead the children of Israel into the Promised Land, and he displayed incredible strength and courage in doing so. He was a mighty man of faith and an inspiring leader, but look what happened:

> *The people served the Lord throughout the lifetime of Joshua and of the elders who outlived him and who had seen all the great things the Lord had done for Israel. Joshua son of Nun, the servant of the Lord, died at the age of a hundred and ten.... After that whole*

generation had been gathered to their ancestors, another generation
grew up who knew neither the Lord nor what he had done for Israel.

JUDGES 2:7 – 8, 10

I find it almost incomprehensible that after living a life of such great faith, seeing countless signs and wonders, and winning so many victories, Joshua and his generation dropped the baton from one generation to the next. By God's grace, they had defeated the Amalekites,[12] crossed the Jordan River on dry ground, seen the walls of Jericho come down, and even seen the sun stand still. Yet after all of these miracles that showed the power and provision of a mighty God, the next generation — an *entire* generation — did not know the Lord or the work he had done for Israel.

What happened? Where was the legacy of Joshua's generation? Were they so busy defeating foreign armies that they forgot to remind their children that it had been the Lord who fought for them? Were they not purposeful about passing those stories on to their children? Did they not encourage their children to encounter God for themselves? Maybe after many hard years of war, the parents dropped their guard, complacently dwelling in cities they had not built and eating the fruit of vineyards and olive orchards they did not plant.

We don't know what happened, but something went horribly wrong. Whatever the gap, it had a crippling effect on the next generation. Whatever the reasons may have been, someone somewhere dropped the baton of faith. They stopped carrying on the baton of faith, and a great big God became so small in the eyes of his people that an entire generation could no longer see him.

Yes, we have a tremendous responsibility. Hand off the baton well and we represent God as big to the world around us. Hand off poorly (or worse yet, stop handing off at all) and we represent God as small to the world. Then all of the ground we have taken can be quickly lost as an entire generation is left unreached.

WHAT DO WE HAND OFF?

As the church, we are entrusted to pass the baton of faith from one generation to the next. Let's quickly revisit what we discussed in chapter 6 in light of this responsibility.

- The goal of the race is to become more like Christ.
- The baton is Christ at work in me and through me to the world.
- The race is the process of becoming like the one I'm running toward, Jesus Christ.

Since our race is focused on Jesus and his work, we'd best turn to him to ensure we understand *his* priorities. What is at the heart of this "work" he wants to do in us and through us? Fortunately, we don't need to guess. Jesus told us in no uncertain terms. A teacher of the law asked him this question:

> *"Teacher, which is the greatest commandment in the Law?"*
>
> MATTHEW 22:36

Jesus' answer has come to be called the Greatest Commandment.

> *Jesus replied: "'Love the Lord your God with all your heart and with all your soul and with all your mind.' This is the first and greatest commandment. And the second is like it: 'Love your neighbor as yourself.'"*
>
> MATTHEW 22:37 – 39

It's clear, then, since Jesus says this is the *greatest* commandment, that our top priority is to love God with everything we are and to love our neighbor. *Love is the work of Christ* — both in us and through us to the world. And knowing that we can be slow learners, it's fair to say that learning to love God — so completely, so entirely that we do so with every fiber of our heart, soul, and mind — is a lifelong process. *Christ in us* has a lot of work to do! We are capable of loving God only because he first loved us. His priority, his work in us, is to continually transform our ability to love God and love our neighbor to an even greater level from whatever level of ability we have at the moment. (This is why we never retire from the race as long as we live on this earth.)

After his resurrection, before he ascended to heaven, Jesus made a second crystal-clear statement about his greatest priorities. We know it as the Great Commission.

> *Go and make disciples of all nations, baptizing them in the name of the Father and of the Son and of the Holy Spirit, and teaching them to obey everything I have commanded you.*
>
> MATTHEW 28:19 – 20

My observation is this: the Great Commission is clearly the logical outgrowth of the Greatest Commandment. If we love God with all that we are, then we want to enjoy him and be with him and live in his presence forever. Am I right? If the deepest and most all-encompassing love of our life is God, what could be more important than living in his presence every day of our lives on earth and for all eternity?

So likewise, if we love our neighbors as ourselves, we want them to know and enjoy that same thing; we want them to know God, enjoy him, and live in his incomparable presence all the days of their lives on earth and for all eternity. True?

Therefore, the more the Greatest Commandment grows in our lives (the more we love God and neighbor), then the more the Great Commission grows in our lives (the more we want to invite others into living for and with God now and forever).

Do you see the critical link here?

If we love, then we want to disciple — to lead others to Jesus and teach them to follow him. If we disciple, then we must love. We cannot do the one without the other.

I want to propose a radical thought for you to consider.

I believe that *every* baton God gives us, no matter what it might be, puts into practice one or the other or both of these priorities of God. The work of Christ in us, his work in our own lives and through us to the world, fulfills either the Greatest Commandment (to love) or the Great Commission (to make disciples) or both.

Annie's batons certainly reflect these two priorities. She is now her husband's helpmate as together they build the body of Christ in Greece. And she continues her acts of mercy and service in A21. She is living out God's love for a broken world in need of a Savior and his love for his people. Every baton she carries is one of Christ at work in her and through her. Every baton she hands off multiplies Christ's work into the lives of others, where it will do the unstoppable work of Christ in their lives and through them to the world.

"Sometimes we get that 'I know this baton is for me' feeling when the baton gets placed in our hand," Annie said. "We know it was destined to be. Other times (which is the majority of my experience), it feels like a cold, metal, foreign object that slowly gets warmed as we run. Yet each baton I've carried has the ultimate purpose of pushing back the darkness and advancing the kingdom of heaven. We build the church, we fight injustice, but our eyes are always fixed on Jesus and his finish line."

The same can be true for you. Every baton you carry has the potential to push back the kingdom of darkness and advance the kingdom of heaven. As you spend your life running time and again back into the exchange zone with your eyes fixed on Jesus, you too can strive to hand off as many batons as possible, exponentially multiplying your impact on this world.

MASTERING THE HANDOFF

A beautiful chain reaction began on the cross two thousand years ago, and, through a series of batons handed from one runner to another, generation after generation, you were brought into your race. In order for that chain reaction to continue from you to countless others, everything hinges on your willingness and ability to make the handoff.

When you excel at the handoff, you've learned to be a coach and a cheerleader as well as a runner. One of the greatest challenges in the divine relay is learning how to do a smooth handoff. Surely we learned that from the USA women's 4 x 100 relay team.

In leading teams all over the world for many years, I've experienced the challenges of the handoff, and I've discovered that the following principles help ensure a seamless handoff.

Good-bye to bottleneck and hello to multiplication.

What are some clues that it's time for a handoff? First, you need to be vigilant in prayer, trusting God to lead you. When you're maxed out on your capacity — overstressed and overworked — that could be a flashing alert that it's time to multiply your efforts through a handoff. Otherwise you become a bottleneck and hinder the growth that could happen.

For instance, I've seen moms form informal babysitting co-ops so they can have time to run errands or volunteer at a local ministry, and, in the process, they open the door for building relationships with other moms that allow for even more baton passing. Or consider the time-strapped man who hires a local teen to help with the yard work and so creates the setting to casually sow into the teen's life the truth and love of God. Look for clues that you've hit your maximum capacity, and welcome those clues as opportunities to make a handoff.

Good-bye to ownership and hello to stewardship.

It can be hard to let go of a baton, especially something you've created and poured not just your hours but also your heart into. Our ministry can be like our baby.

I know what it's like to be handed a new baton and feel like I'm running off into the abyss, unsure where I'm going. When I was first handed the baton of fighting human trafficking, I thought, *I don't know how to do this*! But as we receive and run and truly *own* the baton we are given, we figure it out and get it running smoothly. How easy to slip into wrongly thinking that we now "own" that ministry. It's funny, but I've learned that when we say this, we can almost bank on a handoff coming soon. Why? Because we never own the work of God. We are simply stewards of it. You must be able to keep your eyes on the bigger picture, on God who is choosing, calling, preparing, and empowering. We need to run in such a way that we are always on the lookout for the one we can invite into the work so it might multiply. Commit yourself to keep building the team rather than building up your own little empire.

Good-bye to control and hello to change.

Once we've handed off a baton, it becomes somebody else's responsibility, and they are going to put their own flavor on it. It's going to look a little bit different. It may be improved — at which point you'll have to keep your ego in check. It may be dramatically changed — at which point you have to remember it is God's ministry, not yours. God's plan is to grow you in your ability to let go and trust him, our team coach, with the outcome. Do you find yourself tempted to think, *But I can do it better; I can get it done faster*? That's a great time to grow your teaching and coaching skills. Sure, at first, you excel beyond the beginner, but take the long view. If you train well, then that person can run while you accomplish new work, and that person will multiply many times over. Remember, God is going to multiply whatever he is given.

Trust him in every handoff. The runners of the next generation will not look like you, act like you, think like you, dress like you, or speak like you. They are supposed to be *like God*, not you! Welcome the change that new runners bring.

Good-bye to insecurity and hello to humility.

You need to guard your heart so you don't get insecure, so that you don't in any way hinder anyone. Recognize when your identity has become too caught up in your role. This is as true in organizational handoffs as it is in family life and relationships. Be honest with yourself if you fear that the one you are about to hand off to may excel beyond what you accomplished. Submit that to God and move on, focused on God's finish line rather than your ego. Remember, your identity is in Christ, not in what you do. It is a constant challenge, which is why so many people can't let go because they can't separate who they are from what they do. And if they think it all depends on them, then it's not healthy, because it should depend on God. We must learn to celebrate that ministry goes on beyond us rather than secretly hope that it falters so that everyone will think we are irreplaceable. Beware of the enemy, who will toy with your pride to thwart the race. Keep your eyes focused on Jesus. He is the hero, not you and not me.

Good-bye to the past and hello to the future.

Where once I did nearly everything myself in the ministry, today things have grown so far beyond me that I do more vision-casting and setting up infrastructure, and then I step back and empower others to do everything that I personally do not need to do. I know that if I've done it right and in the timing of God, the person who takes it on from me will be able to take it further than I could have. If you truly believe that what God has for you *next* is better than where you are now, and that what he has for the next person coming up is better for the race and for them, you will be eager for the next person to excel beyond what you did. This outlook keeps your ego under control and your humility in good working order, because it is never about me, me, me. It is all about God, God, God. It is God who prepares, who raises up, who anoints and appoints. Our job, as we carry our baton, is to stay tuned to God's leading whom to pass the baton on to — and when.

FROM ONE GENERATION TO THE NEXT

Following these principles should allow us to avoid the disastrous example of Joshua's generation. I have a passion for all of us to grasp this truth: We must not fail to pass the baton of faith to the next generation. We must see life as a series of receiving and releasing batons so that we carry faith further down the track to others.

Wherever you are running, be it in family, business, school, ministry, or the workplace, you can hand off batons of faith in every relationship you encounter in your daily interactions. In fact, the single most important place to run is into the lives of the people God has placed in your circle — your children, your spouse, your brother, your sister, your coworkers, your friends, and your neighbors. Every single one of us who is a part of the church of Jesus Christ has a responsibility to carry the baton of faith to our own generation and ensure that it goes to the next generation. Are you a parent? Consider this:

> *These commandments that I give you today are to be on your hearts. Impress them on your children. Talk about them when you sit at home and when you walk along the road, when you lie down and when you get up.*
>
> Deuteronomy 6:6–7

Nick, the girls, and I take time each day to share with one another all of the great things that God is doing in our own lives and ministry. As our girls learn to see God at work, they will see God's faithfulness in the past and will learn to trust him with their future. If something comes up at school, we talk about it from Jesus' perspective. As they participate in loving God's Word together, speaking to God together, personally interacting with him, praising him, and taking their needs to him, it will all become a natural part of their lives. Even as Nick and I nurture our marriage, we are handing off trust and sacrificial love to each other while modeling it for our girls. The media, educators, and politicians do not have the responsibility to carry the baton of faith to a generation — nor will they. It is our job.

Of course, carrying the baton to the next generation is not only for parents. Every aspect of your life — every decision you make and every action you take — serves to either keep the relay moving or, conversely, to hinder the race. Passing the baton of faith is as easy as taking time to invest in people's everyday lives like Jesus did with the disciples.

No matter how fast-paced your life is, you can always find a way to turn the normal, inconsequential moments into eternal moments. Traveling with a coworker on business? Use that time sitting in an airport between flights or during a car ride to share an answer to prayer you've experienced. What about a coffee break? Going shopping with a friend? Casually talk about a Bible verse that struck you or a life concern you've taken to God in prayer. Make the sharing of life a transfer of spiritual truth.

Do you see that suddenly everything becomes important because your life is no longer only about you but about all those who have come before you and are destined to come after you? Your life is meant to declare God's works.

When we live morally pure lives in an immoral world, we are handing off our witness that God, our creator, knows how we are best designed to live. When we live a God-first life in a world of competing options, we are handing off the value of placing God as our first priority. When we practice creation care, we tell the world that we love God's world. When we forgive one another instead of harboring offense, we are handing off grace. When we serve the least of these, we are handing off the baton of compassion. When we fight for justice, we are handing off the baton of the incalculable value of each life created in the image of God. And when we stay planted in our local church, we are embedding ourselves in the body of Christ, where we can be encouraged, admonished, mentored, and in turn do the same for others.

I hope you are catching a vision of how all that we do is an opportunity to either carry the baton of faith until we put it in the hands of the next generation or drop the baton so it does not get to them. It is so tempting to make short-term decisions that will result in our own immediate gratification, but in order to fulfill our purpose, we must keep an eternal perspective. Faith is always only one generation from extinction, and we are the ones entrusted with carrying the baton to our generation and handing it off to the next. Let's determine that we won't drop it.

IF NOT YOU, THEN WHO?

If we do not declare the greatness of our God working through the ages, then who will? In God's timeline, this is our moment in history as the body of Christ. Let me rephrase that. In God's timeline, this is *your* moment as a member of the body of Christ. As you run, as you hand off one baton after another, never lose sight of God's cause. Every baton you are given is given so that you might give it to others. Will you run into the exchange zone and hand off the baton of faith for the next generation?

May you gain so much momentum while the baton is in your hand that you help catapult the next generation into all God has for them. May they run faster, harder, and greater than any generation before them so that the world may know our God and see his work in action. After all, the baton of faith is all about the glory of God being revealed on this earth. We run to his glory, for his glory, shining his glory so that others may see his glory.

One generation commends your works to another; they tell of your mighty acts. They speak of the glorious splendor of your majesty — and I will meditate on your wonderful works. They tell of the power of your awesome works — and I will proclaim your great deeds. They celebrate your abundant goodness and joyfully sing of your righteousness.

PSALM 145:4-7

CHAPTER 9

FUELED BY PASSION

"Chris, my car is broken down, and I won't be able to do the 11:00 a.m. lecture on effective evangelism at the Bible college today. Can you please cover for me?"

Without thinking, I said yes to my friend John, not knowing that this unexpected baton was going to be a defining moment for my life. I didn't have any time to think about what I was going to teach the first-year students, but I couldn't let my friend down, so I raced out the door of the youth center and ran the three blocks to the Hillsong Bible College.

I stepped into the classroom flustered at the thought of potentially teaching the worst lesson of my life because I was so unprepared. Playing last-minute substitute wasn't a comfortable role for me, but fortunately, I could draw on my four years of experience in the field doing youth ministry. To this day, I have no recollection of what I taught that day, but something did happen that was more than I had ever bargained for.

A few weeks later, while at my gym for my 6:00 a.m. swim, I noticed that a young man who had been in the classroom on the day of my lecture was already swimming laps. He looked about my age, late twenties. We nodded and smiled, and I thought little of it until the next day and the next. It seemed he was becoming a regular.

Casual nods became hellos and smiles, and before long, I learned that his name was Nick Caine. He'd worked in the financial markets, he told me, until he had a revelation that his life was meant for more than getting up every day, paying a mortgage on a lovely home in the suburbs, and accumulating wealth. So he quit his job and became a cab driver on a quest for meaning. One day, he ran into a former colleague who invited him to a church meeting, and instantly Nick responded to the message of the gospel. Radically, overnight, he had enrolled in Bible school.

Today when Nick tells this story, he simply says, "I fell in love with the teacher." Yep. He loved me before I loved him.

Fortunately, he didn't tell me that at the pool or I'd have hightailed it out of there in a hurry! I considered myself president of the Singles-Till-Rapture Club. I thought that by accepting the baton of ministry to lead, teach, and serve students, I would never have the baton of marriage. I had assumed that a woman could not be both a traveling evangelist and a wife, and frankly, that suited me just fine as I was still carrying around a lot of baggage from my past.

As I carried on my normal life over the next weeks and months, Nick set out on a passionate pursuit of me. At first, I was clueless. I just assumed the guy liked to swim, not that he had ulterior motives. Next, he started showing up as a volunteer at our youth center and did whatever he could to be in my vicinity. Obviously, he had done his homework. He said he figured that if I got to know him, I would not be able to resist him. (Confident, wasn't he?) I guess he was right, because before long I found myself hoping I would bump into him. He had a sharp mind, a keen wit, passionately loved Jesus and the church — and did I mention he was cute? He asked me out to coffee. He was determined to pursue me. And, oh, was he good at it!

Somewhere along the line we transitioned from intense conversations about ministry while working side by side at the youth center to conversations over coffee, then picnics. I still don't know how that happened. Maybe it was the day he showed up with an invitation for a picnic at the park. "I didn't know what you like to eat," he explained as he opened his trunk, revealing four different types of bread, six different cheeses, ten different meats, and salads in case I was a vegetarian.

What kind of guy would even think like that?

To my surprise, I found myself besotted with him.

Passion is like that, isn't it? When new love invades your heart, you can't resist finding ways to make your beloved happy. The grass looks greener. The sky looks bluer. And the energy! Where does it come from? Suddenly you become unstoppable! You can talk long into the night, go to bed late and get up early, eager to see one another again without feeling the least bit tired.

Convinced it was the will of God, Nick was relentless in his pursuit of me. As we drew closer, I began to realize that the brokenness of my past had built walls around my heart. Nick sensed my pain and worked with me through my healing process. He was patient and undeterred. Being the twelfth of thirteen children, Nick was used to being the underdog and somehow emerging the champion. This was no different, and he did get what he was pursuing.

DRIVEN BY PASSION

When you are passionate about someone or something, you do not take no for an answer. You are unstoppable in your determination to find a way. You get creative. Passion drove Nick to get up at five in the morning to get to the pool before me. Passion drove him to finish his college assignments late into the night so he could volunteer at the youth center. Passion kept him coming back when I would get fearful and push him away. Passion made him wear great aftershave and even buy clothes that both fit and matched!

Passion will enable you to do what you would never do if you didn't have it.

When Nick asked me to marry him, I was shocked. Would God possibly give me both ministry and marriage? Could he? Was this part of my race? I'd believed I could accomplish far more for the gospel as a single woman. I was so focused on maximizing every minute of every day for the call of God in my life, I couldn't imagine making room in my life for a husband and a family.

One night, I was speaking at a youth rally of about a thousand kids. Before I stepped onto the stage I prayed, *Father, if I'm going to go further with this guy, I have to know that I'm going to do more for your kingdom married than I am single. Otherwise, I've given my life to you and I just want to stay single. I have to know. Do I keep dating this guy?*

I sensed God's response to me out of Deuteronomy 32:30, which says, *"How could one man chase a thousand, or two put ten thousand to flight?"*

Chris, God was saying to me, *you can choose whichever one you want. If you don't marry Nick, this is what you will have. You will have one thousand, like tonight. For your whole life wherever you go, I'll use you. But one will chase one thousand to flight. Two will put ten thousand to flight. So if you do marry him, you will have a tenfold impact for my kingdom.*

I called Nick and told him my conviction that if we married, I believed we would have a far greater impact ministering together than I had ever had alone. But ... I would not be a traditional wife. Could he cope with that?

"Christine," he said, "what am I supposed to tell God on judgment day? Am I supposed to say, 'Lord, I'm sorry for all the millions of people who did not hear the gospel because I was too insecure to let Christine go out and evangelize'? That I wanted my underwear washed and my clothes ironed and a nice home-cooked meal every night? So I'm sorry that I never let her go. And I'm sorry that all these people went to hell?"

Nick wanted me to keep running the race. He did not want me to stop or slow down. He simply wanted us to run together. I was too stunned for words and overcome with the gift God had given me in this man — a man who would join me in ministry. He was so secure in himself and his relationship with God that having a wife in a leadership role in a national ministry was not a threat to him but an honor. He was okay with me, a woman on the stage, and he backstage, a spiritual warrior in our ministry. How could it be that this man, so passionate for the cause of Christ, was also passionately in love with me?

I thought, *Lord, I can marry that kind of man.*

And so I did. That is the power of passion!

Passion enlarged my heart. Not only was I still passionate for the cause of Christ and pursuing my purpose, but now I was also passionate about this amazing man of God. My goal did not change. Together, we would run toward the finish line. It was Jesus and always would be. God did not give me the baton of marriage to drop the baton of ministry; he gave me Nick to help carry the baton of ministry. God gave me the gift of the most determined, committed, selfless, unstoppable man I've ever met. A man so secure in his identity in Jesus Christ and his calling that he could break through the unseen, unrealized walls of my heart and take me deeper into the power of love than I had ever imagined possible.

Here we are two decades and two children later. We are still running our race. Still passionate about each other. Still passionately pursuing the cause of Christ.

Don't get me wrong. We have had ups and downs and challenges to overcome, but our overriding passionate commitment to Christ and to one another has enabled us to keep running this race together when we might otherwise have given up. Passion is not a momentary, fleeting emotion but the fuel of God in us, enabling us to be unstoppable as we run our race and finish our course.

MY FIRST LOVE STORY

Nick loved me and relentlessly pursued me, wooing me in every way he could conceive. As he did, my disinterest in him became interest, and my enjoyment of him grew into anticipation of more time together, which brought deeper joy and satisfaction, sparking my desire to be with and invest myself in him. Love was born and grew until it became a powerful, shared love that we both nurtured, and so it has grown even stronger in the years since.

But Nick wasn't the first one to pursue me.

God passionately pursued me. When his love and grace captivated my heart, it awakened in me my own sense of divine purpose and destiny. I wanted to run with God and run toward him. I discovered that his plans for me were for good and not for evil, that he was for me and not against me, and ever so trustworthy. Thus began a lifetime love affair of responding to the love of God by pursuing the One who had pursued me.

His relentless pursuit of me was the starting gun for running my race, and passion for him fuels my continued focus on the finish line. For Nick and me alike, Christ in us is both the source of our passion and the sustainer of our passion. His pursuit of us began before we knew him and continues as we run with him and toward him.

When we aren't passionate about God and his purpose for our lives, the race becomes a "have to" instead of a "want to." The divine relay becomes little more than a series of good works and accomplishments for the purpose of earning God's love and approval. The danger in running sheerly from a sense of obligation is that one day we will decide we don't "have to" continue, and we'll drop out of the race.

But when we start our race knowing we are already deeply loved, valued, and accepted by God, then we are unstoppable as we carry our baton forward from a place of grace. We don't run to perform for or earn the approval of God. We run from the place of already being accepted by God. What we do externally is an outflow of what is happening internally.

KEEPING YOUR LOVE ALIVE

When you are fueled by the love and grace of God, you will have the inner strength required to keep running and not give up when you encounter difficulties and challenges. Every step of your run will be part of the adventure of your love affair with Jesus.

But maintaining that passion is not something that happens automatically.

Passion, you see, is not a feeling. It's a decision, or a series of decisions, that fuels an ongoing love affair. Anyone who has sustained a long and healthy relationship over many years knows that feelings come and go. But decisions can be made and actions taken to consistently fuel our passion. Nick and I nurture our passion by making decisions to spend time together, laugh and play together, listen and share dreams, and meet one another's needs. The same is true of our relationship with God, and yours too. When you know how much God loves you, you run your race from a place of deep security, fueled by this love. It fills you and keeps refilling you through everything, from life's mundane challenges through its trials and storms.

Since passion is the fuel that helps us to run our race, it is crucial that we cultivate ways to keep the passion alive. Circumstances can change and our feelings can change, but I have found that by reminding myself of the following truths and intentionally taking these actions, I can remain consistent in my passion for God despite what is happening around me.

God purchased eternal life for you with the blood of his only Son, so keep your love alive by running your race out of joy, not obligation.

Nothing demonstrates God's love for you more powerfully than the cross. *"You are not your own; you were bought at a price"* (1 Corinthians 6:19 – 20). Jesus wasn't forced to die for you. He wasn't overpowered, outnumbered, or tricked into it. He chose the cross out of love for you. Jesus' passion for you took him to the cross — through the pain, through the humiliation, through the separation from God — and then to the resurrected life he lives to share with you. Now that is passion!

As you run, you express your love back to him. You run not to earn his love but in response to his unconditional, unstoppable love. Run your race as a love gift, for the joy of blessing God. *"For the joy set before him he endured the cross, scorning its shame, and sat down at the right hand of the throne of God"* (Hebrews 12:2). For the joy of it, pour out your life for him.

God loved you before you loved him, so keep your love alive by telling him you love him ... every single day.

God created your inmost being. He knit you together in your mother's womb. He knows the number of hairs on your head. He delights in you and loves your company. He designed you with a purpose and has good plans for your future. There is nothing you can do to make him love you more or less. *"We love because he first loved us"* (1 John 4:19). Now fuel your passion by declaring your love back to him! Tell him you love him. Speak words of love to him every day.

God speaks his love into your life, so read his love letter to you—the Bible—daily.

Nick told me that he loved me. He whispered it. He wrote it. He declared it over and over, and as he did, I drank it in like a thirsty sponge. His love fed me and eventually stirred my love for him. God's love for you can do the same. Do you long to hear his voice declaring his love for you? You can drink in the great depths of his love for you as you abide in his Word daily. There isn't a day that goes by that I don't talk to Nick or connect with him in some way, and I would be crazy to think that my relationship with God should be any different if I want to keep my passion alive. I don't know how else to say this other than to just say it: READ YOUR BIBLE. It is filled with his promises and will fill you with his wisdom to keep you on track with your destiny. My prayer for you is that you may *"experience the love of Christ, though it is too great to understand fully. Then you will be made complete with all the fullness of life and power that comes from God"* (Ephesians 3:19 NLT).

God rejoices over you with singing, so keep your love alive by giving him your thanks and praise.

He loves you so much he has brought untold joy into your life. *"He will take great delight in you; in his love he will no longer rebuke you, but will rejoice over you with singing"* (Zephaniah 3:17). He has given you eyes to see the colors of this world and ears to enjoy the sounds of birds singing, babies laughing, and music that stirs your soul. Respond by delighting him with words and music of praise and gratitude. I believe that music is an untapped treasure chest that can carry the heart of God, shift the atmosphere of a room, and help change our perspective in the midst of our circumstances. The Bible says to *"enter his gates with thanksgiving and his courts with praise"* (Psalm 100:4). When you find it difficult to connect with God or stir your passion for him, start by thanking him for all he has done and then find a praise and worship song to sing as a declaration of his promise in the midst of your current situation. I cannot tell you how this simple act has helped me to keep running so many times throughout my Christian walk.

God heals your pain and brings healing into your life, so display your love to him by bringing healing to others.

Nick recognized the brokenness in my heart from my years of being abused and sought to ease my pain and bring healing. In so doing, he walked alongside me as I slowly learned to move beyond my past. You can love God back by looking for opportunities to be the hands and feet of Jesus, seeking to ease the pain of the broken people in this world. The more you love others, the more your passion for God will grow. *"Dear children, let us not love with words or speech but with actions and in truth"* (1 John 3:18).

Use the previous five practices as your starting point for keeping your love affair with God alive. And here is one other idea. Have you ever written out the story of God's relentless pursuit of you? Try it. As I was composing this chapter and wrote out how Nick won my love, I felt compelled to go running to him with a smile in my heart and to tell him all over again how grateful I am that he never gave up. Remembering our story re-stirred my passion. Telling it to others amplifies my passion. The same is true of our relationship with God.

THE WIDE-OPEN, EXPANSIVE LIFE

Did you know that the definition for *passion* is "an intense desire or enthusiasm for something"?[13] The word *enthusiasm* comes from two Greek words: *en* meaning "in or within," and *theos* meaning "God."

Yes! Passion means "in God." Sound familiar? *Christ in us! Christ in you!* What better understanding of the source of passion could there be than understanding that passion comes from having God's presence within us?

Christ in you means that you alone do not keep your God-passion alive. Have you ever tried to manufacture passion where it doesn't exist? It's similar to a cheerleader trying to whip an apathetic crowd into enthusiasm. If the cheerleader works hard enough — and especially if something exciting happens in the game — she might succeed or she might not. But passion for the purposes of God is not something we manufacture within us under our own power. It is *supernatural*. Passion is the inner spark provided by God's Holy Spirit that ignites you to your God-given purpose.

So open your life to the continual infilling of the Holy Spirit. Do you remember what Jesus told the disciples about the coming of the Holy Spirit after the resurrection, just before he ascended into heaven? *"I am going to send you what my Father has promised; but stay in the city until you have been clothed with power from on high"* (Luke 24:49).

That promised gift was the Holy Spirit, and it is the Spirit who *clothes us with the power from on high*. What a powerful description of the role the Holy Spirit plays in our lives. His passion fills us as he comforts us, teaches us, empowers us, counsels us, convicts us, and intercedes for us. So open up wide. Continually invite God's Spirit to pour passion into you. He will — and then life will pour abundantly out of you into others, wherever you go. And you will discover a life filled with unstoppable passion, because it will be fueled by God himself.

Paul writes a beautiful invitation to that kind of passionate life.

Dear, dear Corinthians, I can't tell you how much I long for you to enter this wide-open, spacious life. We didn't fence you in. The smallness you feel comes from within you. Your lives aren't small, but you're living them in a small way. I'm speaking as plainly as I can and with great affection. Open up your lives. Live openly and expansively!

2 CORINTHIANS 6:11 – 13 MSG

The wide-open life is about waking up every morning and knowing that *you were born for this day*. When I look into the eyes of my husband and children, when I see lives transformed through ministry and love, when I see God multiply what we offer him and make our "not enough" into more than enough, I taste this wide-open, expansive kind of life, and my passion to keep running the race grows.

What is it that drives Olympic athletes to get up early, push through pain, set aside distractions to keep their focus, and maintain their commitment — for *years*? Passion.

What keeps Kalli and all the rest of our A21 staff at locations around the world going day after day, year after year, even though they must repeatedly face the discouragement and emotional pain of seeing bruised and battered young women trapped in slavery? Passion.

What keeps Katja and Favour, once brutalized slaves themselves, from descending into bitterness and instead moving toward recovery and forgiveness? Passion.

What kept the early Christians hard at work spreading the gospel, even though they saw their fellow believers imprisoned and tortured and knew that they themselves could be thrown into stadiums, where they would be torn to pieces by wild animals before a crowd fired by bloodlust? Passion.

Passion fuels the mother to stay up all night caring for her feverish child. Passion fuels a father to work two jobs to put his kids through college. Passion fuels a woman to care for her elderly, disabled father. Passion fuels a grandmother to set aside her dreams to care for her fatherless grandchildren. Passion drives the human heart to persevere through hardship when nothing else will keep us going.

Jesus' life on this earth was the ultimate picture of the passionate life. He embraced children, delighted in doing the will of the Father, healed the sick, loved the lost, helped the marginalized, dined with friends and neighbors, and gave his all to run his race. When I see Jesus and his cause, I glimpse the wide-open, spacious life he wants you and me to enjoy.

Today I am more passionate than ever, full of vision, full of faith, full of love, full of hope, full of purpose, full of zeal, and full of dreams, willing to pick up more batons and let go of others as I do the Lord's work. May the same be true for you. May you know no greater thrill than running your race with your eyes fixed on Jesus. He is so worthy of our all.

I am convinced that neither death nor life, neither angels nor demons, neither the present nor the future, nor any powers, neither height nor depth, nor anything else in all creation, will be able to separate us from the love of God that is in Christ Jesus our Lord.

ROMANS 8:38 – 39

CHAPTER 10

THE MAKING
OF A CHAMPION

"Nick, everything you've told me has my head spinning," Phil said. He was a young man about to complete his Bible college certificate in ministry in Sydney, Australia. "But I think there has been some mix-up. You've got the wrong guy. I wonder if there is another guy named Phil who was supposed to get the message to meet with you. I'm not applying for a job. I'll be heading back home to Denmark as soon as I finish my studies. My plans are already made."

"No," Nick replied with confidence, "you're the one I wanted to meet with. I've heard about you through the college staff. Chris and I know you are passionate about building up the church of Jesus Christ. We've heard about your integrity, your character, your compassion, and your relentless heart after God. We see you as a young man with enormous potential and wholeheartedly believe you're the one to lead our new initiative in Greece."

Phil shook his head, trying to absorb all the shocking information Nick had been pouring out for over an hour about human trafficking and the plans to open the first A21 safe house. Phil had received a text message the day before from the church office, asking him to meet with Nick. They'd never met before. Phil couldn't imagine the purpose of the meeting, and he'd come filled with curiosity as to why he'd been summoned. He felt overwhelmed with the horrific information he was hearing. As Nick shared staggering statistics and played heart-wrenching videos of trafficked women recounting their stories, Phil had recoiled at the depravity at work in human hearts, but he couldn't fathom why Nick had called him here to tell him such things. And then — the shocker. Nick wanted Phil to move to Greece and accept the position as head of the A21 efforts there as soon as he completed his certificate in just two months.

"Nick," Phil protested, "you want me to go to Greece? I've never been to Greece. I don't even speak Greek. I've never even heard of human trafficking before today. You want me to start an organization with you? I've never started an organization before. I don't know anyone there. You want to entrust me with your name, your money, your integrity, and to start this thing from scratch in Greece? You don't even know me! Why me?"

Why me, indeed. Throughout the history of the divine relay, God has surprised people with unexpected and seemingly illogical batons. Phil had had a baton thrust toward him. But as much as his mind dismissed this baton as some mistake, his heart was moved. Until this meeting, he'd been certain he knew God's will for his life — a church-planting effort in his home country of Denmark. But now his soul was stirred with a fresh awareness that maybe God's plans for his life were different from the road map he'd already marked out for himself. Phil found himself squirming at the thought. He'd have to tell his extended family that he wasn't coming home. He'd have to lay aside his dreams and move to a foreign land in the throes of deep financial and social upheaval.

"Nick, I'll pray about it," Phil said as Nick handed him piles of research on human trafficking to review.

"All the way home and all that night my soul was screaming at God, 'What are you doing, Lord? This is not part of my plan,'" Phil said. "But somehow I knew this was God's leading. As I began reading for myself the evils to which women and children were being subjected, I was just consumed. In preparation for ministry, I'd been praying for months, *Lord, break my heart for what breaks yours. Not my will but yours be done with my life. I will go wherever you send me.* It had been easy to pray that way when I was certain that God's plans aligned with my own, but now my heart was breaking in new ways."

Phil already had a heart for people, but now that he knew of this evil in our world, an intense sense of injustice rose up within him. "I was filled with a righteous anger at what the enemy was doing," Phil said, "and I knew I was being given an opportunity to do something about it. There was no way that I could turn that down. This offer from Nick was not a coincidence. It had been placed in my hands. The only question facing me was what I was going to do with it."

What followed is a marvelous example of everything we've discussed in this book. Phil accepted that baton and was off and running immediately. Did he feel ready? No. Did he feel qualified? No. "I thought of a long list of reasons why I was not qualified for this job," Phil said. "I didn't have adequate education for the job. I didn't have experience in organizational leadership. I didn't know how to work with politicians and law enforcement, especially in a foreign land and foreign language. I didn't know the first thing about how to set up and run a safe house for women who've been enslaved and brutalized. I'm not a counselor or psychologist or educator."

He saw huge obstacles looming before him, monumental challenges. But in spite of them, Phil knew the Lord of the divine relay well enough to know that God had been preparing him as only God can. He knew that it was God who qualifies his runners, not man. "Suddenly, I realized God had been preparing me for this new direction. He wasn't taken by surprise even though I was. This was just crazy enough to be God! I saw his fingerprints all over it and knew he was calling me to say yes to this opportunity."

Phil could accept this baton because he'd been growing on the run for a long time, fueled by the passion of God's love for him. Phil was in love with the God of the impossible. So he embraced his place, willing to be uprooted from his comfort zone and transplanted into a foreign culture to do a job for which he had no training or experience. He already knew the mystery of Christ in him and was dedicated to receiving and releasing the batons God brought his way. Though only in his early twenties, Phil was a living testimony to the unstoppable power of God at work in him and through him to the world.

Phil hit the ground running. He went from his first conversation with Nick in May to a research trip to Cambodia in June, where he saw, firsthand, victims in a shelter there. His first encounter with these victims left him shocked and shaken. He saw their bruises and wounds and was struck by the indisputable evidence that God had just placed him on the front lines of the battleground described in Ephesians.

> *Our struggle is not against flesh and blood, but against the rulers, against the authorities, against the powers of this dark world and against the spiritual forces of evil in the heavenly realms.*
>
> EPHESIANS 6:12

Phil had been called to war.

The fear in the eyes of the victims and their shattered self-worth brought home the truth that engaging in this battle meant entering the brutal world inhabited by cruel, violent criminals. It was a sobering encounter, but though it sickened him, it emboldened him as well.

In July, he landed in Greece to set up the A21 office, and within a month of receiving approval to operate a transition home, they received the first victim into care. From the start, the enemy attacked him with thoughts of fear and inadequacy. Eager as Phil was to set the captives free, he faced the obstacle that they were hidden and locked away, unable to escape for help or severely punished if they did. He would have to find ways to reach the victims he'd come to help.

He and our new team invaded the enemy's territory but were met with corruption and the insidious presence and power of the traffickers. Not only were the victims in danger, but so was the team working to rescue the victims and expose the traffickers. For the first time in his life, Phil experienced the fear of being in real physical danger. The traffickers were not playing games. Their livelihood was being threatened, and they were threatening in return. The danger was real.

At night the screams of the women in their care awakening from nightmares pierced the quiet. The severity of their physical wounds sickened the team. The threat of hopelessness and despair drove them to their knees as they each had to face the enemy's attacks on their hearts and minds in addition to the seemingly never-ending obstacles they confronted.

The words of Romans 8 came alive as never before.

What, then, shall we say in response to these things? If God is for us, who can be against us? ... Who shall separate us from the love of Christ? Shall trouble or hardship or persecution or famine or nakedness or danger or sword? ... No, in all these things we are more than conquerors through him who loved us.

ROMANS 8:31, 35, 37

Phil became all the more dedicated to his new calling.

WE ARE AT WAR

We are in a spiritual battle. The enemy does not want us to fulfill our destiny. Phil understood this, and when the threats came, when bribes and intimidation and corruption were discovered, when court delays endangered witnesses and convictions, when team members were stalked, he recognized the work of the enemy. He knew that when you say yes to God and join his cause, overnight you may go from running with the wind to running against the wind and not even know how or when the wind changed.

Knowing that we have an enemy is one thing. Finding yourself face-to-face with that enemy's work is another. I won't sugarcoat it. Trials and storms will come to you. Obstacles will rise up. Challenges will multiply. There is always a fight in the exchange zone. The enemy comes at us hard. His goal is to stop us!

Why? Because he has so much to lose. If he can persuade us to drop our batons, to stop running, imagine all the future handoffs and releases he would prevent. If he can tempt us to walk out of the race, not only will our spiritual lives grow stagnant but our influence in this world will diminish as well. If he can make us regret receiving one baton, he hopes we may not accept the next. If he can weaken one part of the body of Christ, he knows the whole body will suffer.

God's divine relay threatens the enemy's territory, and he will not go down without a fight. If you have any doubt of that, just read of his insidious attempts to tempt Jesus at the onset of his ministry[14] and of his work in Judas.[15] If he is bold enough to try to take on the Son of God, he won't hesitate to do his best to thwart us, the followers of Christ.

But here is the spectacular truth:

Greater is He who is in you than he who is in the world.

1 JOHN 4:4 NASB

Jesus overcame the Evil One. The enemy is *already* defeated. And what's more, God uses the enemy's tactics against him. What the enemy intends for evil, God uses for good. Yes, Satan used Judas to betray the Lord, but God intended for Jesus to stand trial and be condemned to death. Yes, Satan used the scheming of Jesus' enemies to have him crucified but, in so doing, Satan fulfilled God's plan for securing eternal life for all who believe in Jesus. Satan loses! God wins!

I see this at work in my own life. The enemy sought to destroy me through abandonment and abuse, but God rescued me to make me a rescuer. What the enemy intended for evil, God used for good.

So what happens when the enemy attacks a runner in the divine relay? What happens when the fiery darts come at us, when trials beset us, when storms come, when opposition hits? Do we allow these attacks, trials, and storms to stop us? No! God uses every single trial to our benefit, for our good.

Phil wasn't stopped by the enemy's attacks. Every obstacle and challenge became a tool in God's work to make him an unstoppable champion. Phil grew stronger. He led our team in setting up a stellar safe house, then a legal office, then an anonymous tip line that opened the floodgates to reach more victims and gather more intelligence to win more court battles. The US State Department, in its Trafficking in Persons report, named Phil as a hero, one of the ten most influential people in fighting trafficking, and Secretary of State Hillary Clinton personally presented him the award.16 Today Phil is our global operations manager and our trouble-shooter, because in overcoming the seemingly insurmountable obstacles and weathering the storms, he has been strengthened.

Do you see how God uses obstacles, trials, and the enemy's attacks to make us stronger when we refuse to stop running our race? Because Phil refused to stop, there are traffickers in jail and victims freed and more runners carrying more batons in the race. God is building champions.

With greater strength, we can handle increased responsibility — greater batons. As we do, as our impact increases, the opposition grows fiercer, which in turn, if we persevere, increases our endurance. All the time God is building us and strengthening us. As we trust him and see his faithfulness, we can run harder and faster on the next leg and the next.

From my vantage point, one of the most beautiful realities is that more often than not, a champion never self-identifies as one. The greatest champions I know are ordinary people who trust the true champion, Jesus, to come through and do what he said he would do. They run. They obey. They follow Jesus anywhere and everywhere, and no matter what challenges they hit, they keep on running.

Phil is one of those champions.

CHAMPIONS FIND GOD'S STRENGTH IN THEIR OWN WEAKNESS

It would be so much more comfortable if God would keep us in our "strength zone," wouldn't it? But God keeps thrusting us into our "weakness zone" because it is only in our weakness that he is made strong.

> [Jesus] said to me, "My grace is sufficient for you, for my power is made perfect in weakness." Therefore I will boast all the more gladly about my weaknesses, so that Christ's power may rest on me. That is why, for Christ's sake, I delight in weaknesses, in insults, in hardships, in persecutions, in difficulties. For when I am weak, then I am strong.
>
> 2 CORINTHIANS 12:9 – 10

We are finite beings, but we serve an infinite God. The good news is that God is never limited by our limitations. Whenever he calls us to step out of our comfort zone and into the exchange zone, it is because he wants to do something in and through our lives. God didn't choose Phil because Phil was big enough and strong enough and smart enough to do this enormous work. He chose Phil because he knew Phil would be unstoppable in recognizing that *only God* could do this work — and would follow him, trust him, and become his hands and feet and mouthpiece in a work that only the God of the impossible could do.

When we remember it is about God's strength and not our own, then we are more willing to trust him and allow him to use us for his purpose. Phil and his team faced their weaknesses in the midst of their obstacles and trials (more about this in the next chapter). Champions see their weaknesses, then see God's strength revealed in the face of their weakness, and so grow in endurance and perseverance.

Now, here is the critical question: How do we increase our willingness to trust in God's strength when our own weakness is so glaring that it captures all our focus? Let's turn to Peter's championship training and find out.

TRAINED TO BE A CHAMPION

The raging wind battered the small boat and, in spite of the strong men straining against their oars to reach land, the disciples were getting nowhere. It was about 3:00 a.m. The sky was pitch black. Their aching muscles screamed for rest, but they kept at it, wrestling with their oars to at least keep the boat headed into the waves so they wouldn't capsize. When they'd pushed off from shore just a few hours before, the water had been calm and the boat seemed to offer what they needed most — rest and solitude from an exhausting day unlike any they had ever known.

They'd just learned that John the Baptist had been executed. Sickened with grief, they had planned to take the day off to rest and grieve. After hearing the crushing news of his cousin's death, Jesus had led the disciples to withdraw to a quiet place to rest, outside of town. But the locals — about five thousand men plus women and children — had discovered Jesus' location and soon swarmed them, so they'd spent the entire day ministering to the crowds. We read in chapter 2 about how Jesus miraculously fed everyone in the crowd with no more than five loaves and two fish. When that miracle was complete, Jesus told his disciples to "immediately" get into the boat and go to Capernaum on the other side of the lake while Jesus stayed behind to dismiss the crowd and then go off by himself to pray.

Put yourself in the wave-soaked robes of the disciples and consider the depths and the heights they had experienced that day. The unjust death of John the Baptist must have affected them deeply. But sandwiched between the tragic news of John's beheading and this frightening windstorm that was tossing their boat around like a toothpick, they'd seen Jesus perform a mind-boggling miracle. Now, only hours later, they faced this storm.

Let's focus in on Peter.

Keep in mind some critically important events in Peter's life that had come before this moment. His first encounter with Jesus had been on Peter's own boat when Jesus told him to toss his empty nets back in after a fruitless night of fishing. Peter, amazed by the miracle that ensued, had to shout for some other fishermen to help him haul in the nets overflowing with fish. Peter began to follow Jesus that day, and ever since, Peter had listened and watched as Jesus' ministry unfolded. The lame walked. The blind could see. The ill were healed. Evil spirits were cast out. Peter even looked on as Jesus healed his mother-in-law, bedridden with a fever. Once when Jesus was with his disciples on a boat and a raging storm hit, Peter and his fellow disciples feared for their lives, then watched in awe as Jesus calmed the storm in a moment.

The crowds had grown, and with them Peter's faith had grown. His understanding grew. His dreams and hopes for the future grew. His love for Jesus grew. And as Peter continued to follow, he developed into a leader among the disciples. His understanding of who Jesus was had been growing bigger and deeper.

So you see, by the time of this storm, Peter was no novice in witnessing miracles. Now you are about to witness one scene, one more step, in the making of this champion.

Straining against the oars with every muscle, Peter must have longed to have Jesus there in the boat with him. *If only the Lord were here*, he must have thought, *he would calm this windstorm before our eyes, like he did before.*

And then they saw him.

Let's pick up the story in Matthew 14:25 – 29.

Shortly before dawn Jesus went out to them, walking on the lake. When the disciples saw him walking on the lake, they were terrified. "It's a ghost," they said, and cried out in fear.

But Jesus immediately said to them: "Take courage! It is I. Don't be afraid."

"Lord, if it's you," Peter replied, "tell me to come to you on the water."

"Come," he said.

Then Peter got down out of the boat, walked on the water and came toward Jesus.

I love it! That's Peter. He was all in. Or should I say all *out*, because Peter was so ecstatic and relieved that the Lord had come to them in the darkness and the danger, so awed that Jesus could walk on top of the very water that threatened their lives, that he wanted to walk on water with his Lord. So he climbed out of the boat and started walking while the wind was still raging!

But when he saw the wind, he was afraid and, beginning to sink, cried out, "Lord, save me!"

Immediately Jesus reached out his hand and caught him. "You of little faith," he said, "why did you doubt?"

MATTHEW 14:30–31

Why *did* he doubt? Hadn't Peter witnessed miracle after miracle, even a breathtaking one mere hours before? Yes, he had. But at this point in Peter's faith, yesterday's miracles didn't yet outweigh his fear of today's dangers. He took his eyes off of Jesus and saw, instead, his own frailty.

Can you relate? I believe we all can.

The danger of drowning was real. Peter wasn't tucked away in safety, contemplating the truths in some scroll of Scriptures. He wasn't sitting at the feet of Jesus on a sun-warmed hillside, considering the meaning of a parable or how the truths of Jesus' teaching might apply to his life. No. In a surge of ecstatic faith, he'd climbed out of the boat with his eyes fixed on Jesus, but when his face was being slapped by the stinging spray of crashing waves, it suddenly occurred to him that there was nothing under his feet but water. Peter's fear was, from a human standpoint, totally understandable. He didn't feel any solid rock under his feet. In fact, his feet were disappearing down into those waves in a hurry.

I'm thinking of Phil again. He'd climbed out of the boat — he'd boarded a plane for Cambodia. But face-to-face with the broken and bruised flesh-and-blood victims like the ones he'd just agreed to help, he didn't feel solid rock. He felt his own inadequacies. When faced with the harsh realities and real evils and dangers of this world, we humans have a tough time taking refuge in spiritual truth.

And this is exactly why we *need* storms and trials in our lives if our faith is to grow.

UNTESTED FAITH IS FRAGILE

It's no coincidence, of course, that the windstorm "just happened" to occur on the heels of the miracle of the loaves and fish. Keep in mind that Jesus is omniscient. He knew when he loaded the disciples into the boat that this storm would come. He *chose* to be on land, a distance from his disciples, when the storm hit. He *chose* to allow them to be tossed about, knowing their fears would surface. He *chose* to display his power to walk on water when their fears were at their height. And he *chose* his words carefully when he said to Peter, "You of little faith, why did you doubt?"

Jesus used Peter's moment of weakness as a teaching moment. He'd exposed Peter's lack of faith and then proved himself faithful in the face of it.

In Mark 6:51 – 52, a parallel rendering of the Matthew 14 account, we catch on to what Jesus was showing them in the middle of that storm.

Then he climbed into the boat with them, and the wind died down. They were completely amazed, for they had not understood about the loaves; their hearts were hardened.

They had not understood about the loaves — the miracle they'd witnessed just hours before. Sure, they knew Jesus had miraculously multiplied the food, but they had not grasped how that act had revealed the deity of Jesus — his identity as being one with God, and thus his omnipotent power over the physical world. *Their hearts were hardened*, meaning that their capacity to perceive and understand was hampered.

However, though the multiplication of the loaves hadn't opened their eyes, a few hours of fear must have softened those hardened hearts, because when Jesus came strolling along walking on top of the water, they got it.

And when [Peter and Jesus] climbed into the boat, the wind died down. Then those who were in the boat worshiped him, saying, "Truly you are the Son of God."

MATTHEW 14:32–33

The storm had done its work!

The darkness, the danger, the physical distance between them and Jesus had all revealed where their faith was weak. Then, and only then, did Jesus climb into the boat with them and quiet the storm.

Like Peter and the other disciples, you and I need to see the power of Jesus more than once. Before Peter's walking-on-water night, he'd experienced God's power to some degree, but like Peter, until our faith is tested through challenges, obstacles, trials, and storms, it cannot be stretched to new lengths, deepened to new depths, nor grown to new heights. Faith must be tried to its limits before it can grow *beyond* those limits. As long as we are on this side of heaven, God is not finished with his work in us or through us. His goal is to keep making us more like him — to transform us from timid children of faith into unstoppable champions of faith. And one of the tools he uses to grow and transform our faith is trials.

TRIALS ARE THE ULTIMATE STRENGTH-TRAINING EXERCISE

Consider it pure joy, my brothers and sisters, whenever you face trials of many kinds, because you know that the testing of your faith produces perseverance. Let perseverance finish its work so that you may be mature and complete, not lacking anything.

JAMES 1:2–4

Let's admit it: Pure joy is not our natural response when we face trials and the weakness they reveal. Think about the struggles in your own life, now or in the past. Betrayal. Illness. Financial stress. The loss of a job. An unexpected tragedy. Relational disasters. Family upheaval. The powerful message of this verse is clear — bad news can be faced with great hope. Whether your trials came as a result of your own brokenness or poor choices, or because of the choices of someone else, or by an act of nature such as a flood or an earthquake or a tornado, or as a consequence of living in a fallen world, you have reason, even while grieving and hurting, to be joyful.

Why?

Because trials test your faith, and every test reveals where you are weak.

Is it bad news when your weaknesses are revealed? No! The weaknesses are there inside us, whether we know it or not. Better to have them revealed so we can acknowledge them and, with God's work inside us, see our weakness rooted out and strengthened.

Just look at Jesus' response to Peter. He shone the spotlight on Peter's doubt with his question, "Why did you doubt?" And what did Jesus do next? Immediately he reached out his hand and caught Peter, then climbed into the boat with him, then calmed the storm. He showed Peter that his fears and doubts were unfounded. He proved his faithfulness to Peter to dispel that doubt. His test of Peter's faith thus did its work in building Peter's faith for the future.

But notice this in the James 1 verses: the building of perseverance must not be passive on our part. It is not God's work alone. Our *response* to our trials and tests is critical to the process.

God gives us two commands: *consider* and *let*. We are to "consider it" pure joy. This requires us to make a deliberate decision about how we view the trial, believing that God is at work to make us stronger. We must "let" perseverance do its work by working with God, not against him, in the face of our trials. This is not our natural response, but it is the faith-filled response we are called to make.

We, like Peter and Phil, have choices to make in the face of life's trials, and what we choose has a direct bearing on whether we are growing into champions of faith. Peter responded just as we must if we want to find joy in the face of our trials: he reached for Jesus. He could have sunk to his armpits and then, spitting mad, swum back to the side of the boat, cursing Jesus for allowing him to sink. But he didn't. He cried out to Jesus, and Jesus reached for him. Phil could have decided he'd made a huge mistake and flown home to Denmark. But he didn't. He reached for God's strength and carried on in Greece. And do you know what happened next?

More tests. More trials. Obstacles. Roadblocks. Hurdles. Of course! Phil was in championship training — and he still is. What else would we expect? We face greater and greater trials as we keep heading back into the exchange zone for more and more batons. But God uses the tension, complexity, and challenge of doing his kingdom work to transform us into his champions.

God is the wisest of coaches. We can trust him that even in the midst of pain, he is at work for our best eternal interest. Our job is to persevere, trusting his perfect work in our lives.

YOUR WALK-ON-WATER MOMENTS

Champions understand that God uses every trial — every hurdle and obstacle — as our spiritual workout to build our strength and endurance. This is why Jesus, knowing that within hours he would be arrested, flogged, paraded through the streets, and crucified, said the following words to us:

> *"All this I have told you so that you will not fall away. They will put you out of the synagogue; in fact, the time is coming when anyone who kills you will think they are offering a service to God. They will do such things because they have not known the Father or me. I have told you this, so that when their time comes you will*

remember that I warned you about them.... I have told you these things, so that in me you may have peace. In this world you will have trouble. But take heart! I have overcome the world."

JOHN 16:1 – 4, 33

Do you hear him? Take heart! Be of good cheer! Consider it all joy! Such times are when you will experience firsthand that greater is he who is in us than he who is in the world. Such times can be your walk-on-water moments. When winds of storms come — and we know they will — we will ride the storms on his wings. When the challenges, trials, and obstacles come, he will catapult us to the next level of faith.

Between the disciples and Jesus that windy night, there was darkness, danger, and distance. Ever been there? Your storm is raging "here" and Jesus seems to be over "there." But it doesn't matter how dark the night, how distant the location, how dangerous the circumstances. When you are straining against the oars — contending with your trials — remember that just as Jesus knew the disciples were in trouble and came to them, he knows when you are in trouble, when you have had enough, when you need strength and courage. He knows when to calm the storm and when to ride it out with you. And he knows exactly how to use it to make you stronger.

Climb out of that boat with your eyes fixed on Jesus. And if you falter, cry out to him, reach out to him, knowing he will catch you and climb into your boat. When the time is right, he will calm the storm. But he will choose the time — when your weaknesses have been revealed, when your doubts have been exposed. Then he will step into your weakness with his strength and will prove your doubts are unfounded and that he is faithful and trustworthy.

With this confidence, as we face the hurdles and obstacles in our divine relay, we can say, with Peter,

In all this you greatly rejoice, though now for a little while you may have had to suffer grief in all kinds of trials. These have come so that the proven genuineness of your faith — of greater worth than gold, which perishes even though refined by fire — may result in praise, glory and honor when Jesus Christ is revealed. Though you have not seen him, you love him; and even though you do not see him now, you believe in him and are filled with an inexpressible and glorious joy, for you are receiving the end result of your faith, the salvation of your souls.

1 PETER 1:6 – 9

CHAPTER 11

OUTRUNNING THE PASSION-SLAYERS

"What do you see?" my professor asked as he projected a picture of a small black dot in the middle of a very big white screen. I was sitting in Psychology 101 during my years at Sydney University.

We all responded immediately: "A black dot."

I was excited, thinking, *If all of the questions are as easy as this one, this course is going to be easy!*

The prof looked out over the class and paused for several seconds before he asked again, "What do you see?"

Thinking he must not have heard us properly the first time, we repeated even more loudly: "A black dot!"

Again he paused ... and then asked the same question a third time.

Now he had my attention. And when still, on the third try, none of us provided the correct answer, he explained — and gave me a lesson I will never forget. "You were all so focused on the little black dot in the center of the screen that none of you noticed the dominant image on the screen: the large white space covering the screen top to bottom, left to right."

I couldn't believe I had missed it. Suddenly it was obvious. There was far more white space than black dot. Whatever I chose to focus on had my attention. There is *always* much more white space than there is space covered by little black dots — we simply need to recognize and focus on it.

In class, that idea seemed like an easy notion — easier than it has proven to be in life. Because the harsh reality is that the black dots of our lives — the trials, challenges, disappointments, obstacles, and hurdles we face as we run — will naturally draw and consume our attention. Our enemy would love to get us to focus on those black dots and convince us they define and shape our lives and determine our destiny. But in the divine relay, we are to fix our eyes on Jesus. He is the "white space" of God's power at work in the universe, and the trials we face are but a tiny speck, a black dot, in comparison. As we learn to focus on the vastness of God's eternal, amazing work on this planet, those black dots will cease to blemish our lives.

Phil experienced the truth of this. The trials Phil had endured after accepting the baton of fighting human trafficking could have stolen his passion and derailed him from his race. He could have focused on the black dots — the painful circumstances our team encountered, the fear of danger and of team members' inadequacies and personal failures, the discouragement of unmet expectations, relational strife, weariness, hopelessness, and the power of the enemy's opposition. All of those trials were real and could have slain the passion that drove him and our team forward in their race.

But he and our team became unstoppable by keeping their eyes fixed on Jesus, the author of their faith and the one who would carry it to completion. They are champions in the making and are learning on the run to focus on that which is far bigger than those black dots — the white space of God at work. The more they've practiced, the stronger they've grown, and Phil would tell you they are still practicing.

It's not easy to go the distance, is it? There are casualties in this race. People will disappoint you. You will fumble and fail at times. Most things will take longer than you think. The circumstances will be painful. The battles can be fiercer, the mountains higher, the rivers wider, and the terrain rockier than you anticipated. The goals set before you will seem another inch away no matter how close you get. I told you I wouldn't sugarcoat it!

Not one of us intends to get derailed, but we must recognize that we could be if we do not heed God's call to keep our eyes fixed on Jesus. As we put our championship training to work, the enemy will do his best to drain our passion and wear us down to the point that we drop out of the race. The enemy who kills our passion steals the fuel that keeps us running.

THE PASSION-SLAYERS

I've observed some common ways the enemy works to draw our focus to the black dots of our lives and sow discontentment. I call these tactics the passion-slayers. My list is by no means exhaustive. Far from it. But I've found that believers who've learned to conquer these tactics are well-equipped to handle just about anything the enemy can throw at them. Here's my list:

- Negative circumstances
- Fear
- Failure
- Unmet expectations
- Relational strife
- Weariness
- Opposition
- Hopelessness

Let's examine each of these passion-slayers and retrain ourselves to focus not on the black dots but on the vast white space of God's power at work. As we learn to see how small those black dots are in comparison to God's greatness, we will come to understand that they are not interruptions to God's work at all but are simply trouble spots — trials — where God is actively at work.

Do you see how that understanding changes everything? Suddenly, instead of being distracted and discouraged by those black dots, we can connect those black dots to see the picture that emerges — the picture of God at work in this world!

Negative circumstances: See the invisible work of God in your visible circumstances.

Few things can be as discouraging as negative circumstances. What events and situations in your life have threatened to derail you? A crisis in your family or at work? A medical diagnosis? Maybe your finances are depleted and the car breaks down, or a treasured friend is moving away, or a leader you've come to trust announces he's leaving your church, or you are stretched beyond your limits already and your brother needs to move in with you, or your daughter's been arrested and you need to step in and parent your grandchildren. Whatever the circumstances may be, when they loom large and threaten to deplete your faith, it's time to do what Paul says in 2 Corinthians 4:18: *"We fix our eyes not on what is seen, but on what is unseen, since what is seen is temporary, but what is unseen is eternal."*

What a wonderful way to view the world! But how do we see the unseen? The psalmist exhorts us: *"Oh magnify the Lord with me, and let us exalt His name together"* (Psalm 34:3 NKJV). When we use a magnifying glass, we are not making the object bigger; rather, we are amplifying our ability to see it for what it really is. Think of the telescope in an observatory. To the naked eye, distant stars are but a tiny speck of light. But in reality, they are huge. We never want our understanding of God to be limited to what we can perceive within the confines of our limited vision;

we want to see him for how huge he really is. So boost the power of your lens to see how huge God really is. He is always everywhere. There is always more of God than our pain and disappointments. The real question is not "What's gone wrong?" but "What good is God doing that I cannot yet see?"

One way to boost your ability to see God's hugeness is to *worship him regardless of your circumstances*. I often have to look up and declare his greatness, and only then does my heart start to shift. Even though the circumstances may not have changed, my perspective has changed because I choose to *magnify* the Lord, his Word, and his promises above the circumstances that I can see. And that changes everything.

Easy for you to say, you might be thinking. *You don't know what's going on in my life*. That's true, I don't — and I don't mean to in any way belittle the giants you may be facing. But I *do* know — and I want you to know — that God is bigger than any circumstances, no matter how daunting. Problems that seem overwhelming, that threaten to deplete your passion, can be made small in the light of God's greatness. They become tiny black dots on the immense — the infinite — white screen of God's work in the universe. By looking at your circumstances through the lens of God's eternal truth rather than through the lens of your temporal circumstances, you won't allow external circumstances to steal your internal peace. Remember, the size of that dot is determined by the focus you give it, so magnify the Lord so you can see that God is bigger than the circumstance you face and is at work through it.

Fear: See trust grow where fear reigned.

Fear surged through Phil when he stood face-to-face with the first victim who came into the care of the brand-new A21 shelter in Greece. He said, "Until then, I had read about victims, I had even witnessed them firsthand in Cambodia. But now I was standing there face-to-face with a broken woman. Her life was now my responsibility, and I felt so out of my boat."

Sure, Phil knew he had a team to help him, but ultimately he felt the weight of all that responsibility on him. A precious life needed to be rescued out of a horrendous situation, and he felt responsible to be the one to make sure that she was safe. "It was my watch under which she was to become whole and healthy," Phil explained. "I felt such a heavy burden of responsibility, and I prayed, *Lord, I'm not prepared. How can I possibly be ready for this? What if I fail her?*"

Have you ever struggled with questions such as, How can I possibly meet such needs? The task seems too great and I feel too small. What if I'm not up to the task? What if I start down this road and fail?

Do you hear the whispers of the enemy? What if, what if, what if? It's important to recognize that voice so that you know a trial when you face one. Instead, listen to God's voice: *"For God has not given us a spirit of fear, but of power and of love and of a sound mind"* (2 Timothy 1:7 NKJV). The moment you taste fear, focus on the good news that you've just seen the territory where your faith is about to grow. Like Peter standing on the turbulent water, reach for Jesus, recognizing that though you are not trusting God to meet your needs, you *want* to. Our God is a good God who has great eternal plans for you that nothing and no one can thwart.

Do you have doors of opportunities before you that you are too fearful to walk through? I almost missed going to college because I feared my family's reaction and tradition. I almost refused to preach around the globe because I was pathologically afraid to fly. I had also wondered, *What if I fail? What if I am mocked? What will my friends or family say?* Fear is just a feeling that will pass. It is not reality. Christ at work in you and through you is reality. When you learn to see areas of fear as places where trust is about to grow, fear gives way to courage.

Failure: See the building of your character through failure.

Let's face the truth — we will falter, fumble, and fail, but failing at something does not make you a failure, nor is it final. The race does not end when you fail at something; the race ends for you when you stop getting back up and continuing to run. Proverbs 24:16 tells us, *"For though the righteous fall seven times, they rise again."* The key is refusing to quit. Do not stop. Never. Ever.

Our ideas of "failing" and "succeeding" in this race are often built on our false assumptions about the ultimate goal of our race. Remember, it is not so much about what we accomplish for God, but that we are becoming like him. Failure, when offered to him, builds our humility and our reliance on him. Champions persevere through failure. They fall and they fail. Like Peter, they sink, but then they reach. They hide, but then they show themselves. They run, but they return. They strike out in impetuous anger, but they accept rebuke and submit. Champions are never perfect. Only Jesus is perfect. But champions press on. They persevere. They will not be stopped.

All of us have at one time or another dropped one or several of the batons entrusted to us. But the good news is, it is never too late to pick up the baton where you are and once again run your race so that you can finish your course. Remember, God is bigger than any of our past mistakes. Jesus has redeemed our lives so that we can all have forgiveness for our past, a fresh start today, and a hope for the future. Don't believe the lie that you have been disqualified from this divine relay somewhere along the way. Instead, pick up your baton, look to Jesus, and start running your race again. You are not out of time. God has given you enough time to do all that he has called you to do. While there is breath in our lungs, while our heart is still beating, there is always a hope, and there is always a future. It is never too late for Jesus to complete the unstoppable work of salvation that he started in you.

Unmet expectations: See great expectations rather than unmet expectations.

Phil arrived in Greece expecting to set captives free. But not only were they enslaved, they were hidden away, afraid to come, or unaware of the help of Phil and our team. Listen to how God used these unexpected obstacles to open new doors. They could have become a passion-slayer, but instead they became a source of even greater expectations of what God would do next.

"That first year we went in expecting that all we had to do was open a home and we'd be flooded with women wanting help," Phil said. "However, when 99 percent of victims are never rescued, that means very few come out on their own accord, and even fewer come into care facilities. The enemy kept these women imprisoned as much by fear as by locked doors." So Phil and our team went to the police expecting that if they made themselves available, the police would send them victims. They were wrong. They quickly realized that the police didn't have the intent or the resources to be proactive about combating human trafficking. The job A21 had come to do was far bigger and more complex than Phil expected.

God, Phil prayed, *we need to get creative with new approaches to reach those we're here to help.* God answered. Phil explained, "We tried to put ourselves in the position of a trafficked victim. Where did she go? What did she see? Who would she interact with? How could we find ways to infiltrate her world and come alongside her?" Those questions generated a huge list of people our team had not expected to need to network with, such as hospital staff, detention center workers, lawyers, border control personnel, and more. Again, the job was bigger and harder than expected, but they pressed forward.

I want you to notice what happened here, because Phil's story illustrates exactly what we've been discussing. Every one of the team's unmet expectations pushed them to expand their reach. So *Christ in us* — Jesus at work through his runners as they ran with their batons — was touching the lives of all the people the team networked with. This is the mystery at work. This is Christ at work *in* Phil and our team, making them champions of faith, while also working *through* Phil and our team to carry the light of the gospel.

I can barely sit still at the thought of it! This is what we are made for! This is the divine relay! This is the great race you are running in! So if you find yourself struggling with unmet expectations, cast them aside and keep running with great expectations to discover what God had in mind all along.

Relational strife: See the opportunity for harmony rather than strife.

Internal conflict can shut things down and slay your passion far quicker than any external attack. As long as you are working with human beings, you will contend with grumblers or be in danger of becoming one. Misunderstandings will occur. Egos will flare. Selfish ambition will rear its head. (And it may be in you! It certainly has been in me at times.)

I have great news for you: Every time strife hits, you are being handed a beautiful opportunity to love like Jesus. People-loving is precisely the work of Christ in you, so count on growing in it. God's Word spells out the guidelines. *"Make every effort to live in peace with everyone and to be holy; without holiness no one will see the Lord. See to it that no one falls short of the grace of God and that no bitter root grows up to cause trouble and defile many"* (Hebrews 12:14 – 15).

We are pilgrims together on a journey with twists and turns. Live at peace with others, with no bitterness, so that others may see God at work in you. Love one another. That doesn't mean warm fuzzies; that means the deliberate work of 1 Corinthians 13. Love is patient. Love is kind. Loves does not envy. If you have any questions regarding your part in resolving conflict, read that chapter in the Bible — first, obey it in your words, actions, and decisions, and ask God to help your heart to follow. Whenever strife begins, thank God for the opportunity to see the power of his love in action, then commit to addressing it and resolving it in love. On God's vast canvas, strife is a tiny black dot, but what a beautiful picture it can become of forgiveness, grace, and love.

Weariness: See God's rest in the face of weariness.

In Matthew 11:28, Jesus beckons us, *"Come to me, all you who are weary and burdened, and I will give you rest."* When you are weary in body, mind, or soul, you must have rest. Weariness can steal your passion and leave you depleted and ineffective. You must actively take care of yourself, and doing so requires that you examine the reasons for your tiredness. In our fast-paced entertainment and social-media-driven world, we can become depleted without even realizing it. Are you getting the sleep you need? Are you taking a Sabbath? Even the Son of God rested, so surely you must, too.

Sometimes we are weary because we don't know how to say no. You cannot do everything that everyone asks you to do. Remember, the body of Christ works together to do God's work. Are there handoffs you've been reluctant to make? Are there burdens hindering you that you must throw off? Perhaps you are driven to control what is not yours to control. Relinquish what is not yours to carry. You may have a blind spot in this area and need wise counsel. Then seek it! Galatians 6:9 says, *"Let us not become weary in doing good, for at the proper time we will reap a harvest if we do not give up."* Even though we need to have goals, objectives, strategies, performance indicators, and so on to help us get to where we believe God wants to take us, we cannot twist God's arm or make something happen in our own timing or strength. Our due dates are often different from God's appointed times, so do not get discouraged or disappointed. Stay faithful, trust God, and get some rest!

Opposition: See God use opposition to achieve his goals.

Phil at first felt intimidated by the evil he saw at work behind human trafficking. He learned how well-organized the criminal traffickers were. He heard stories of collusion between traffickers and government officials. He learned of death threats and danger, of the dismal chances of arrests and convictions. He caught the big picture of how internationally connected traffickers are and of how women are smuggled, with many not surviving transport. He thought he'd understood evil before, but as he looked into the eyes of those trafficked women, as he saw the physical and emotional scars, he knew he was standing face-to-face with an evil more twisted, more powerful, and more dangerous than he'd ever known. He discovered he'd entered a war zone, and he'd just been sent to the front lines.

At times, the power of the evil, the corruption of the governments, and the ominous influence of the organized traffickers all appeared to have the upper hand and seemed to be winning. Had Phil become discouraged, had the presence of such evil stolen his passion, he would have left defeated, given up. The passion-slayers would have won. But Phil and our team kept their eyes and their prayers focused on our omnipotent God. Phil refers to one particular trial against a major trafficker as "a real nail-biter," but the team appealed to believing friends on several continents to pray for victory. Phil reports, "The trafficker was sentenced to fifteen years in jail and a fine of 108,000 euros! This was a landmark case and the first of its kind in A21 history. But not the last. The opposition may have been great, but our God was greater." See how God uses opposition to achieve his goals, and this will put the black dots of your opposition in clearer perspective.

Hopelessness: See God's way when we see no way.

Hopelessness occurs when we no longer see any way forward. If ever you find yourself there, be aware that you've lost sight of

God's great white expanse. God is not in trouble, in crisis, broken, sick, or impotent. He is still in control — he is omniscient, omnipresent, and omnipotent. He is still on his throne! So step back. Refocus. Acknowledge that God has a way when you see no way. Everything we see that appears to be a giant, a roadblock, the end, is but a tiny dot on the infinite white space of God's work in the universe!

We must refuse to stop running! Why? Because our hope is in Jesus, who is at the end of the race. Reach toward that hope. Focus on what it takes to finish and win. Like Peter, cry out to Jesus, focus on him, reach for him to save you, and you will find yourself back in the boat, Jesus by your side, the winds gone, the waters calmed, and you and Jesus back on course for the next day of running, the next baton, the next handoff. Because this race is the Lord's, and it's not over yet. God wins! As his runner, as long as you persevere, you win. Every day pray, *Lord, even if I cannot see you, I hope in you and trust you.* Hebrews 6:19 – 20 says, *"We have this hope as an anchor for the soul, firm and secure. It enters the inner sanctuary behind the curtain, where our forerunner, Jesus, has entered on our behalf."*

I am so grateful that my impact on this world has not been limited to my confidence in myself. At times I have felt inadequate, unable, and unqualified. Yet these limitations have not stopped me from stepping into God's purposes for my life, because by choosing to grasp each baton God has given me, I have ultimately learned that it is not about my UN — it is about the ONE.

If Phil, and Kalli, and Kristen, and Annie, and Nick and I, and the rest of our team had focused on the impossibility of rescuing the roughly thirty million who are trapped today in human slavery, we would never have rescued the ONE. The one Katja. The one Favour. The ones whose names you do not know. Every time we start a new office in a new country, we are guided by the hope of success, not the fear of failure. Setbacks are a chance to learn and excel. We refuse to accept that human trafficking is too hopeless for God and instead have chosen to believe that with God, all things are possible. We must never become overwhelmed by the enormity of a problem, but instead, we must continue to hope in the power of God to bring change, transformation, freedom, healing, and hope. God makes a way when there is no way.

THE SECRET OF CONTENTMENT

God's Word provides us with a powerful secret that will enable us to outrun the passion-slayers. We can learn to be content in the midst of our trials. Learn the secret of contentment, and you can endure for the long haul.

The apostle Paul must have been a master of the secret of true contentment.

I have learned to be content whatever the circumstances. I know what it is to be in need, and I know what it is to have plenty. I have learned the secret of being content in any and every situation, whether well fed or hungry, whether living in plenty or in want.

PHILIPPIANS 4:11–12

Notice that contentment didn't come naturally to Paul. It doesn't come naturally to any of us. Paul said, "I have *learned* to be content." This passage has so much power because of where Paul was when writing these words. He wrote not while vacationing on a Greek island resort but while sitting in a prison, being persecuted for his faith.

True contentment has nothing to do with our external circumstances but rather with our internal dependence on Christ and our confidence in the work he is doing. Do you remember the mystery we discussed in chapter 6? As long as we are running in obedience to him, *Christ in us* is the one at work in every step of our race.

He gives us strength to do whatever we need to do and whatever we need to be in the moment. Contentment, then, is found in Christ alone — nothing more, nothing less, nothing else. Contentment is found in the presence of Jesus, not in the absence of difficulties.

This means that when discontentment creeps into our thinking, it is a red flag that we've taken our focus off of Jesus and set it on the black dots of our circumstances. When that happens, do an instant course correction; immediately place your focus back on Jesus. Choose to see that *Christ in you* is at work. His work is unstoppable! The black dots capturing your attention do not distract Christ from his work. In fact, he can use every one of those black dots to take his work in you one step further. He can use them to make you stronger, wiser, faster — to shape you into the champion runner who will one day cross the finish line. When we learn this secret, we understand that our ability to focus on Jesus will bring us contentment.

Being content and confident in God as he equips us to do his work in us and through us, our passion for God and his work will grow.

WE PRESS ON FOR THE PRIZE

In the divine relay, God is achieving his goals in us and through us. Once we've experienced the surge of the unstoppable force of God working through us, we want even more. Once we've discovered the secret of seeing those potential passion-slayers as nothing more than God's opportunity to defeat the enemy and complete his good work, then we are compelled to run all the harder.

God wins, not the enemy! Our confidence comes from Christ. In him you can deal with anything. In him you can survive any test. In him you can overcome any obstacle. In him you can find contentment, no matter what tactics the enemy throws at you. You can do all things through Christ Jesus who strengthens you.

No promise is too hard for God to keep.
No prayer is too hard for God to answer.
No problem is too hard for God to solve.
No person is too hard for God to save.
No mountain is too big for God to move.
No need is too great for God to meet.
There is nothing our God cannot do!

Be aware that the enemy will form a weapon and launch that weapon against you. But God is on your side, and nothing can hinder his plan as long as you do not give up. We will never know what we are capable of in God's strength if we don't run our way through every obstacle, hurdle, and trial to find out. Push through the wavering of your faith until you stand firm in unwavering faith. Yield no ground to the passion-slayers. Choose patience with yourself and your circumstances, knowing that God is at work in you and through you, and he will succeed in his goal. It is this confidence that will take you all the way to the finish line.

"No weapon forged against you will prevail, and you will refute every tongue that accuses you. This is the heritage of the servants of the Lord, and this is their vindication from me," declares the Lord.

ISAIAH 54:17

CHAPTER 12

THE WINNER'S CIRCLE

Nick and I stood in the breathtaking Cologne Cathedral, the largest Gothic church in northern Europe. We had come to this beautiful city to speak at a leadership conference and couldn't resist the opportunity to see this official world heritage site. One of the most well-known architectural monuments in Germany, it is still the country's most visited landmark, with more than twenty thousand visitors a day.

I am one of those people who love to read the story behind monuments, so Nick went to grab an espresso while I satisfied my historical curiosity. I read that construction started in 1248 and took until 1880 to complete. Nothing great is built overnight. This magnificent cathedral was bigger than one generation. In order to build such a grand cathedral, more than ten generations had been willing to sacrifice and toil without seeing the completed work, each generation leaving its legacy of vision, dedication, and accomplishment to the generation that followed.

Similarly, you and I, as we run in the divine relay, are building something that not only will still be developing as we come to the end of our own lives but will last until the days when this earth comes to an end. Jesus is unstoppable in building his church and expanding his kingdom, and this is a cause that is far bigger than any one person or generation. Each person's and each generation's contributions are important, but we must remember that what we contribute becomes our legacy upon which future generations will build. We are part of something eternal, not merely temporal. Many of us will see the extent of the fruit of our lives only from our heavenly grandstand. We will run our race but will not see the finish line this side of eternity. We must run our race with conviction, mindful of that truth. And when the time comes, we must hand the baton to the next generation and take our seat with the cloud of witnesses to cheer them on. Jesus, the author and finisher of our faith, will watch over and ultimately complete that for which we have invested our lives.

The plans God has for us are so big that it will take you and the generations that follow to comprehend and complete his work.

But the plans of the Lord stand firm forever, the purposes of his heart through all generations.

PSALM 33:11

WHAT LEGACY WILL WE LEAVE BEHIND?

A legacy is far more than just the memory of a person's profession, successes, or failures. It also includes the values that governed a person's life. Some legacies are filled with faith, forgiveness, hope, love, compassion, and generosity and have a profoundly positive impact on generations that follow. Others contain things like anger, greed, racism, bitterness, and rejection and have a negative impact for generations to come. Many legacies contain a little of both. The question is not *if* we will leave a legacy, but rather *what* our legacy will be. Will we leave a legacy by default, or will we consciously choose to leave a legacy that has the power to inspire generations to come?

I believe the quality of our legacy is directly determined by how we run our race. Our race lays a foundation for the next generation of runners. When we choose to live a life that extends beyond ourselves and beyond today, we are showing coming generations that there is Someone big and grand who is worth living our life for and giving our life for. Others are watching and learning from us, so it is crucial that we do not grow weary in doing good, stop running our race, or drop the baton.

Jesus said in Matthew 16:18, *"I will build my church, and the gates of Hades will not overcome it."* Throughout the ages, the enemy has tried to snuff out the flame of Christianity, yet it has always survived. Its legacy lives on because Jesus Christ is alive. The kingdom of God is always advancing, showing the world that the church Jesus is building is magnificent and powerful, and neither the power of hell nor the schemes of humankind shall prevail against it. Jesus cares infinitely for the church. He gave his life for it.

We have the privilege of being a part of the legacy of the church. This is our time in history to arise. We must carry our baton with grace and perseverance, knowing that one day Jesus will return for his bride. As we run our leg of the race, we must always remember that *Christ in us*, who is working in and through us, is even greater *beyond* us, for he has been, is, and shall continue to be working through the ages.

Jesus' legacy of self-sacrifice is the richest, most remarkable, and startling legacy in the history of our planet. He loved us so much that he left the perfection of heaven to become one of us, as described in God's Word:

Have the same mindset as Christ Jesus: Who, being in very nature God, did not consider equality with God something to be used to

*his own advantage; rather, he made himself nothing by taking the
very nature of a servant, being made in human likeness.*

PHILIPPIANS 2:5–7

Once here, he embodied the love and mercy of God, teaching,
healing, and working mighty miracles as he purposefully pursued
his greatest legacy of all — the reason he came to this earth. As
that time approached, he prepared his disciples, and when he knew
they were prepared enough (though they didn't seem ready by
human standards), he led them, of all places, to a garden. He was
almost to the finish line.

THE FINISH LINE

When the Olympic champions we discussed in chapter 1 were
running their relay, the destination they had in mind was the
winner's platform, with a medal of gold hung around their necks.
When athletes compete, they picture their prize, the winner's cup,
awarded in the circle of champions to the cheers of those who
stand in awe of their achievements.

At the beginning of our race, we seldom grasp God's grand
plan and how interwoven, far-reaching, and transformational it
is. Often when new believers accept Christ, they begin with the
focus that the Christian life is all about me, me, me — God saving me from hell, God solving my problems, God and me con-
necting in personal relationship. All good things, of course, but
our earliest steps of faith are merely baby steps. Then we begin
to grow in the knowledge of God, and for many, maybe for you,
this is the point at which we realize there is a race to be run.
We start running.

We run. Reach. Receive. Release. Repeat. We embrace our
place. We catch the rhythm. Life hits us, challenges hit us, we
start doing the hard kingdom work and hit resistance, tempta-

tion, roadblocks, and persecution. Handoff after handoff, we carry Christ in us as he transforms us from the inside out and transforms our world through us. Eventually, we realize we aren't running against the other runners. This is no competition, no place for ego or selfish ambition. We are interconnected to other runners in the divine relay, each doing our part. We see God at work in the midst of all of us, his body, and we begin to grasp the huge scope of what he is doing. We are a team, fueled by passion, all straining in sync against an enemy determined to stop us.

The enemy does not want us to reach the winner's circle. But we push through, we persevere through trials, becoming unstoppable champions as we strive to do our part and glory in what God is accomplishing.

That finish line, however, is mysterious — it's always just out of sight. Maybe we are thinking about that cloud of witnesses and anticipating the slaps on our back and hearing, "Well done, my good and faithful servant." We picture name-engraved trophies, jeweled crowns, and revelry and celebration. And yes, that does await us, but it is still far off. There is more we don't quite grasp.

And then Jesus, just as he did with the disciples, runs us straight into a garden.

NEVERTHELESS

And He was withdrawn from them about a stone's throw, and He knelt down and prayed, saying, "Father, if it is Your will, take this cup away from Me; nevertheless not My will, but Yours, be done."
LUKE 22:41–42 NKJV

Do you see it? Do you see the Winner's Cup? Are your eyes open to this brilliant, knee-knocking, fall-on-our-faces, struck-by-awe encounter with the cup of Christ? We've known *of* this cup all along. We've drunk from it since we first became a believer, the blood of Jesus willingly poured out for us. But until now, we've never grasped that this is *our* Winner's Cup as well.

The Winner's Cup is SACRIFICIAL LOVE. When Jesus surrendered, he laid down his life in holy sacrifice for us. Jesus knew what was coming. The agony. The cost. The sacrifice. He knew the whip would tear the flesh on his back, that the thorns would pierce his brow. He knew that not only would the weight of his body pull against the nails in his hands and feet but that the weight of all the sin in the world would also be laid upon him. In agony at the thought of what was coming, he cried out for another way, another choice. But then in one powerful word — *nevertheless* — he surrendered all to the will of his Father.

For us to accept this Winner's Cup, for us to drink of it, is to lay down *our* lives and pour out *ourselves* in living sacrifice to God.

Therefore, I urge you, brothers and sisters, in view of God's mercy, to offer your bodies as a living sacrifice, holy and pleasing to God — this is your true and proper worship. Do not conform to the pattern of this world, but be transformed by the renewing of your mind. Then you will be able to test and approve what God's will is — his good, pleasing and perfect will.

ROMANS 12:1 – 3

Sacrifice. *Living* sacrifice. The act of giving up all we are and all we have as an offering to our Father. Serving others, loving others, preferring others, living for God's purposes and not our own — this is sacrificial living. This is crucifying our flesh, our self-focused ways, and choosing instead the ways of God: love, joy, peace, patience, kindness, goodness, faithfulness, gentleness, and self-control. We can live in such a way only if we die to ourselves and live instead for him — continuously, no longer conformed to this world but transformed according to his will.

And here is the mystery and beauty of it all: The more we

pour ourselves out in living sacrifice, the more God's love pours into us — oceans of it, overflowing, spilling out onto every life we touch, every baton we carry, every handoff we release. We are filled and refilled with the ceaseless, unstoppable love of God. AND WE RUN!

We run to a world that does not know him but desperately needs him. We run to the Katyas and Favours of this world. We run to raise up new Kallis and Kristens and Annies and Phils. We run to neighbors in distress, to girls locked in brothels, to children in hunger, to friends in pain. We run to brothers and sisters in Christ to encourage them in their races. We run to the next generation and welcome them to the race. We run, fueled by the passion of the fullness of God's love pouring into us and through us to a broken, dying world "so loved" by God that he sent his only Son, who drank the Winner's Cup of sacrificial love.

> *"My command is this: Love each other as I have loved you. Greater love has no one than this: to lay down one's life for one's friends. You are my friends if you do what I command. I no longer call you servants, because a servant does not know his master's business. Instead, I have called you friends, for everything that I learned from my Father I have made known to you."*
>
> JOHN 15:12 – 15

YOUR NEVERTHELESS

In the book of Romans, Paul tells us how urgent it is that we be about our Father's business.

> *Make sure that you don't get so absorbed and exhausted in taking care of all your day-by-day obligations that you lose track of the time and doze off, oblivious to God. The night is about over,*

dawn is about to break. Be up and awake to what God is doing!
God is putting the finishing touches on the salvation work he began
when we first believed. We can't afford to waste a minute, must
not squander these precious daylight hours in frivolity and indul-
gence, in sleeping around and dissipation, in bickering and grab-
bing everything in sight. Get out of bed and get dressed! Don't loiter
and linger, waiting until the very last minute. Dress yourselves in
Christ, and be up and about!

ROMANS 13:11 – 14 MSG

This earth is not our home. Never lose sight of the truth that we are pilgrims on a journey to our eternal home and we are to invest our brief time on this earth in something far bigger than ourselves — something that matters for all eternity. Knowing this helps us to hold more loosely to the comforts of this earth and to reach ever forward to grasp the things of God, willing to say our own "Nevertheless, not my will but yours be done." Wholeheartedly. Frequently.

Kalli says "nevertheless" when she closes her eyes at night and must wrestle with the images of the horrific ordeals she's heard from the girls in the safe house. How can she not picture what they describe when they wake up from their nightmares screaming? Yet when she goes running to their beds at night, she does not regret hearing about the images she struggles to forget. She rejoices that she can wrap her arms around a woman healing from her trauma through the love of Jesus.

Kristen says "nevertheless" as she speaks to educators about lifesaving curriculum while sacrificing her nights and weekends to study for her university degree. She realizes that with the baton she has been handed, earning a degree will make her even stronger for her race. Yet because she accepted that baton, she let go of a full-ride scholarship, making this current season a sacrifice of time and intense energy.

Favour's "nevertheless" is sharing her new Christian faith while continuing to do the hard work of healing and forgiving. She works hard to support herself and live a productive, giving life, and she withstands attacks from the enemy, who loathes to lose her from his grasp. Thieves robbed her recently and took everything of worth in her home, yet she perseveres in trusting God as her provider and protector.

Annie's "nevertheless" is her continued sacrifice in Greece, across the ocean from her family, whom she still misses painfully. She still sheds tears when she connects with her parents, siblings, and nephew through social media, but she wouldn't trade her place in her lane as she thrives as the new wife to her Greek-born, church-planting husband. And she joyfully serves with me in a thousand ways, including poring over every word of this book with her keen editorial eye.

Phil continues living out his "nevertheless" in his willingness to never stop praying, *Lord, break my heart for what breaks yours.* God continues to answer, so Phil sees the horror and despair of the broken bodies and crushed hearts of victims as the still-thriving human trafficking cycle continues. He forever carries with him the image of the little girl in Cambodia whose teeth were brutally kicked in as she was raped. How do you see something like that and still go home at the end of the day and find joy? Nevertheless, Phil gladly keeps seeking out victims to help. He is spurred on by the Lord he loves, who *"for the joy set before him ... endured the cross, scorning its shame, and sat down at the right hand of the throne of God"* (Hebrews 12:2).

Nick and I had a new "nevertheless" experience during the writing of this book. We had known for the past year that Nick's mother's health was declining. This great woman had birthed fifteen children and had a special gift to hold the family together. Nick, as the youngest son and second youngest child, was clearly treasured by his mother. One of the many things that attracted me to him years ago was his love for and treatment of his mother.

Then, a few months ago, while I was speaking at an event in Kansas City, a phone call came that sent our hearts beating wildly. One of Nick's sisters called with the news that his mother had fallen and was rushed to the hospital. In a coma, she was not expected to make it through that day.

Oh, how we longed to be there by her side. But even if Nick had jumped on a plane that very second, there was no way he could possibly get home to Australia in time. It would take at least twenty hours of flying time plus all the additional time clearing customs and security, then the additional miles to her bedside.

His sister put the phone to his mother's ear, and Nick spoke his final words to his mother across the world while she was in a coma. He told her she could go home and be with his dad, who had died twenty-seven years earlier and was waiting for her in heaven. Nick knew he would never see his mother again. Within a few hours, she was gone, and Nick, through his grief, made plans for the long trip home to take part in her funeral.

When we said yes to starting A21 and moving away from Australia, we both left behind aging mothers, all our family, and lifelong friends. We knew that the miles — with our often being on opposite sides of the globe — would take a high toll on precious times with loved ones. But after much prayer and reflection, we still felt Jesus was asking us to start one A21 office, then another, and another, and so it continues. Would we have loved to be there with Nick's mother in those final hours? Yes. But nevertheless. Had we responsibly made provision for our mothers in every way? Yes. Do we both call our families frequently? Yes. Did we ask God to keep Nick's mum alive so he could be there? Yes. Did she still get promoted to heaven before he could get home? Yes. Am I aware that my own mother is not getting any younger? Yes.

Are there moments we consider handing it all over and going

back home to the familiar and comfortable? No. Nick and I continue to say, "Nevertheless, Lord! Not my will, but yours, be done." Yes, life is hard and painful sometimes, but Jesus is good. God's grace is sufficient.

What is your nevertheless?

Over the years, I have learned that we cannot always be doing what we want to do, when we want to do it, or how we want to do it, and still be following Jesus at the same time. There will invariably be many "Nevertheless, not my will, but yours, be done" moments along the journey. We must commit to being about our Father's business at all times, regardless of the inconvenience, risk, or hardship that it brings. His business must always be our first priority.

Your spouse may have abandoned you, but nevertheless you will remain a faithful parent committed to raising godly children. You may be tempted to indulge your desires, but nevertheless you will remain morally pure. You may have the opportunity to misuse your access to funds at work, but nevertheless you choose to live a God-honoring life. You may have been deeply wounded by another person, but nevertheless you will forgive. Your boss may be abusing her power and mistreating your team, but nevertheless your response will be above reproach. You may be tempted to walk away from the ministry where you are needed because of relational strife, but nevertheless you will choose to nurture harmony and remain committed to your calling. You may love your gourmet coffee but nevertheless feel led to use your coffee money to sponsor a hungry child. You may be longing for that next "fix" — be it a substance, a habit, an online site, an illicit relationship, a purchase you cannot afford — but nevertheless you choose obedience and freedom. You lay down yourself and lift up your Lord. You choose to be last and put Christ first. You die to self so that you may live in Christ. Nevertheless!

There is no retirement from the race this side of heaven! Your

passion can be refueled and your weary heart refreshed and re-
nourished. Whatever your story, you are sorely needed. And
what's more, your life will be far richer if you sprint now to your
lane and take your position, once again, in your exchange zone. As
long as you have breath in your body, you can breathe God's love
into this world.

BORN TO WIN

Our first birth destined us to lose because *we were born into sin.*
But because of Jesus' "nevertheless" decision, because he went to
the cross to pay the price for our sin, we have been born again.

> *You have been born again, not of perishable seed, but of imperish-
> able, through the living and enduring word of God.*
>
> 1 PETER 1:23

When we are born again, *we are born to WIN!*

And so, in the victory of Jesus Christ over sin, our eternal victory cannot be stopped. As we run in God's divine relay, we are
running in assured victory. We do not run *for* victory but *in* victory. We are part of Christ's triumphal procession, because Jesus
has already won and his Spirit lives in us.

> *Thanks be to God, who always leads us as captives in Christ's tri-
> umphal procession and uses us to spread the aroma of the knowl-
> edge of him everywhere.*
>
> 2 CORINTHIANS 2:14

What an image! As we run, we spread the aroma of God in
our every action and interaction, and we will cross the finish line,
unstoppable, into the embrace of our eternal Father God.

As you take your place in the body of Christ and run the race you were born to win, you are playing your part in what God is doing on this earth. You are making God and his purposes bigger in your life and more important than the temptation to stay in the comfort of your Christian bubble. You are not falling asleep between the first and second coming of Christ, but instead, you are carrying your baton into our hurting world and so bringing light into the darkest of places.

My dream for this book has been to mobilize you to join in this great divine relay — this relay that started long before you arrived on earth and will last far beyond your days upon this earth. Look around you at what the body of Christ is doing. We are world-changers! Get out of the pew and into your lane. Move into your exchange zone and run with unstoppable perseverance all the way to the finish line.

God has chosen you. Prepared you. Placed you. Now run into your exchange zone, hand outstretched and open, and grasp every baton he brings your way. Discover that not only are you making a difference in the world, but God is making a difference in you. Hand off those batons to others and discover the thrill of seeing God exponentially multiply his work. Inspire your fellow runners to run at their peak through your encouragement and example, and see God's work multiply all the more. The world will be forever changed because of *you*.

I believe that as the members of the body of Christ run side by side in his divine relay, we will draw the eyes and the heart of the world to the incalculable love of God and his salvation. Nothing is as unstoppable as the body of Christ working together, loving and serving one another and our lost, hurting, and broken world while eagerly awaiting the return of our Lord Jesus Christ.

My life and yours have been touched by batons carried from generation to generation before us, and we in turn carry the baton of faith forward into our families, our neighborhoods, our schools, and our workplaces. We will carry it to our culture and every culture on this planet. True victory comes with your lifetime commitment to living in the exchange zone, passing on the baton of faith into the life of one, plus one, plus one ...

Therefore, since we are surrounded by such a great cloud of witnesses, let us throw off everything that hinders and the sin that so easily entangles. And let us run with perseverance the race marked out for us, fixing our eyes on Jesus, the pioneer and perfecter of faith.

HEBREWS 12:1–2

You know what God has called you to do, so run, unstoppable, until the day you cross the finish line and hear the words of your father, *"Well done, good and faithful servant!... Come and share your master's happiness!"* (Matthew 25:21).

Now may the God of peace, who through the blood of the eternal covenant brought back from the dead our Lord Jesus, that great Shepherd of the sheep, equip you with everything good for doing his will, and may he work in us what is pleasing to him, through Jesus Christ, to whom be glory for ever and ever. Amen.

HEBREWS 13:20–21

ACKNOWLEDGMENTS

Writing the acknowledgments is always fun for me, as it means the book is finished and I get to thank all the people who made it possible. For me, the most important people to thank are you, the readers. Thank you for journeying with me through these pages. It has been an honor to serve you.

I am a great believer that it takes a village to do just about anything, and this book is no exception. I am so grateful for my family, who have been incredibly patient with me during the many months of the writing process. There are no three people on the planet I love more than Nick, Catherine, and Sophia. Nick is so supportive in practical ways, ensuring that our very full life continues to move forward as I hibernate. He also threw out some valuable thoughts during the revision process that ended up woven into the fabric of various chapters.

Thank you, Esther Gualtieri, for loving our girls and helping all things at home to work beautifully as I typed away. I cannot thank Cindy Lambert enough for agreeing to be my collaborative writer on this project. I have loved every second working together with you. We certainly lived out the message of the book every step of the way, and we crossed the finish line.

It is my great joy and honor to work with the Zondervan team.

Thank you, Sandy Vander Zicht, for your grace, love, patience, and genius editorial eye. You helped the book become what it is, and your support throughout the writing process helped me to keep going. Also, a huge thanks to Greg Clouse and to Londa Alderink and the entire marketing team. You are always so gracious and passionate.

A thousand hugs and thanks to Annie Dollarhide and Natalie LaBorde for reading every single draft and offering so much helpful and wise feedback along the way. And a huge thanks to Bianca Olthoff, Amanda-Paige Whittington, Erin Bruffey, and Kristen Morse for your help.

Thank you to those who allowed me to tell their stories in the hope that others would be inspired to pick up their batons and run their race. (The events and people I've written about are accurately described. However, due to the potential danger of discovery for trafficking victims, I have changed their names and disguised their identities.)

To all of our staff and team at The A21 Campaign worldwide: I love you and I thank God for each and every one of you.

NOTES

1. *http://www.olympic.org/content/results-and-medalists/gamesandsportsummary/?spo rt=32588&games=2000%2f1&event=32567.*

2. *http://espn.go.com/olympics/summer/2012/trackandfield/story/_/id/8256748/2012 -london-olympics-us-shatters-women-4 – 4x100-relay-world-record.*

3. *http://www.olympic.org/olympic-results/london-2 – 2012/athletics/4x100m-relay-w.*

4. *http://records.unitarium.com/athletic-records. See 400m World Record/women.*

5. Moses' initial protests to God's call are recorded in Exodus 3:6 – 4:14. Gideon's doubts and protests are found in Judges 6. Jeremiah's feelings of inadequacy and the Lord's response to them are found in Jeremiah 1:4 – 10. Mary, perplexed at how she, a virgin, could give birth to the Son of God, was humbled and willing, as recorded in Luke 1:26 – 55.

6. "Human trafficking is the second largest global organized crime today, generating approximately 31.6 billion USD each year. Specifically, trafficking for sexual exploitation generates 27.8 billion USD per year," United Nations Office on Drugs and Crime, 2009, "Trafficking in Persons: Global Patterns," *http://www.unodc. org/documents/human-trafficking/Global_Report_on_TIP.pdf.*

7. "800,000 — Number of people trafficked across international borders every year," US Department of State, "Trafficking in Persons Report: 2007." "Tragically, only 1 – 2 percent of victims are rescued, and only 1 in 100,000 Europeans involved in trafficking are convicted," from United Nations, "UN Agency Calls for Better Monitoring to Combat Human Trafficking in Europe," in UN News Centre, 2009, *http://www.un.org/apps/news/story.asp?NewsID=32575&Cr =human+trafficking&Cr1.*

8. Mark 6:42 – 52; Luke 9:10 – 17; Matthew 14:13 – 32; John 6:1 – 15.

9. 1 Samuel 16:1 – 16.

10. *http://www.youthtoday.org/view_article.cfm?article_id=6036.*

11. Moses' encounter with Pharaoh's chariots at the Red Sea is found in Exodus 14. Joshua's experience of bringing down the walls of Jericho is recorded in Joshua 6. Gideon's defeat of the Midianite army can be read in Judges 7. Peter's walk on water is told in Matthew 14:22 – 32.

12. Exodus 17:8 – 13.

13. *http://oxforddictionaries.com/us/definition/american_english/passion?q=passion.*

14. Matthew 4:1 – 11.

15. Matthew 26.

16. *http://www.state.gov/j/tip/rls/tiprpt/2012/192362.htm.*

STUDY GUIDE

CHAPTER 1

THE DIVINE RELAY

1. Christine uses the metaphor of a divine relay race to describe how the church must work and what happens when it doesn't. "Four champion runners collaborating in the relay are faster than a lone champion runner," she writes. "That's the power of a team."

   - Overall, when it comes running the race of faith, how would you describe yourself? Are you more of a lone runner or a team runner?

   - In a relay, everything hinges on what happens in the exchange zone, that place where we deliver our baton to the next runner. How do you know when you are fumbling, dropping, or ceasing to pass the baton of faith? How do you know when you are handing it off smoothly and well?

   - What recent experiences have you had on the receiving end of a handoff? What baton of faith, small or large, has another runner handed you smoothly and well? What happened—in you or through you—as a result?

2. Which of the following statements comes closest to describing your current condition in the divine relay? Share the reasons for your response.

   ☐ **I am running my race and loving it.** I am refining my run, growing stronger, and perfecting my handoff.

- ☐ **I am running my race but not with the same passion or commitment I once had.** I am still moving forward, but it's more out of habit or routine than passion.
- ☐ **I am running out of steam.** I am winded or limping and don't know how much longer I can keep moving forward.
- ☐ **I have dropped my baton.** I feel disqualified, like there's no point in continuing to run because I've failed in some way.
- ☐ **I've stumbled or fallen.** I've hit obstacles I can't overcome and don't know how to pick myself up or keep moving.
- ☐ **Other:**

3. A passage from the book of Hebrews provides a beautiful image of what it means to persevere as we run the race of faith:

> Therefore, since we are surrounded by such a great cloud of witnesses, let us throw off everything that hinders and the sin that so easily entangles. And let us run with perseverance the race marked out for us, fixing our eyes on Jesus, the pioneer and perfecter of faith. For the joy set before him he endured the cross, scorning its shame, and sat down at the right hand of the throne of God. Consider him who endured such opposition from sinners, so that you will not grow weary and lose heart.
>
> Hebrews 12:1–3

For a fresh perspective on this familiar passage, read it again from *The Message*:

> Do you see what this means—all these pioneers who blazed the way, all these veterans cheering us on? It means we'd

better get on with it. Strip down, start running—and never quit! No extra spiritual fat, no parasitic sins. Keep your eyes on Jesus, who both began and finished this race we're in. Study how he did it. Because he never lost sight of where he was headed—that exhilarating finish in and with God—he could put up with anything along the way: Cross, shame, whatever. And now he's there, in the place of honor, right alongside God. When you find yourselves flagging in your faith, go over that story again, item by item, that long litany of hostility he plowed through. That will shoot adrenaline into your souls!

HEBREWS 12:1–3 MSG

- Imagine for a moment that you are running in an Olympic stadium filled with a cheering crowd. These are your biggest fans! And they are not just ordinary spectators but gold medal athletes of the faith who have already finished their races. As you glance up into the stands, whose faces are you looking for? Who is cheering you on from eternity? For example, you might consider biblical characters, faith heroes or mentors, loved ones, etc.

- What do you imagine these fans from your cloud of witnesses might say to you about your current condition in the race (question 2)? How might they be cheering you on, encouraging you to keep going?

- Now imagine shifting your gaze from the faces in the crowd to Jesus. Knowing that he is *for* you (Romans 8:30–31), what do you see in his face as he gazes back at you?

- As you keep your eyes on Jesus, what teaching or stories from his life come to mind? How does studying him, going over his story again, shoot adrenaline into your soul or help you not to lose heart?

4. The goal of the book is to help you become unstoppable as you run the race marked out for you.
   - What concerns or questions do you have as you begin the journey on which this book will take you? What hopes or expectations are you aware of?
   - Throughout this study, how might you be intentional about being a team runner rather than a lone runner? Consider practical ways to give and receive support, and to challenge one another.

CHAPTER 2

IMPOSSIBLE IS GOD'S STARTING POINT

1. The chapter begins with a dramatic story of rescue. What was your initial reaction to the story of Kalli's 3:00 a.m. phone call with Katja? For example, did it challenge you? Excite you? Leave you feeling uneasy or uncomfortable in some way? Share the reasons for your response.

2. "God's call comes to each of us in every age and stage of life," Christine writes. "He calls us to step out of our comfort zone and into the exchange zone, ready to run for him and carry the love of God and the truth of his power into the lives of others."

   • A comfort zone is a situation in which things feel familiar and we experience little to no anxiety or stress. How would you describe your current comfort zones when it comes to faith and running the race marked out for you?

   • Drawing on your own experience, illustrate the difference between being in a comfort zone and being in an exchange zone. Use the following prompts as part of your response:

      I know I'm in a comfort zone with my faith when . . .
      I know I'm in an exchange zone with my faith when . . .

   • Share a past or recent experience in which you felt God calling you out of your comfort zone into an exchange zone.

Whether it was a call to something small and immediate or larger and long term, what was the risk you felt you were taking? How did you respond, and what happened (or did not happen) as a result?

3. Both Kalli and Katja at one time believed it was impossible for them to make a difference in a global problem, but they became unstoppable when they each carried their own baton and responded to God's call. What impossible thing would you make a difference in if you could? Use one or more of the prompts below to dream big about partnering with God to care for the needs of a broken world.

   The difference I would make in my home is . . .

   The difference I would make in my local community is . . .

   The difference I would make at my school/workplace is . . .

   The difference I would make in my church/faith community is . . .

   The difference I would make to address a societal concern, injustice, or crisis is . . .

   Other:

4. Every race has a starting point, the line that marks the change from inaction to action, from standing still to first step. Kalli's starting point was thinking there wasn't anything she could do about a massive global problem like human trafficking. How would you describe your starting point in connection with your responses to question 3? What thoughts, doubts, questions, or insecurities might keep you standing still rather than taking a first step to make a difference?

5. Take a moment to reflect not just on how *ready* you feel to run your race in the divine relay but on how *willing* you are to run. Which of the following statements would you use to answer this question: *How willing are you to run with your baton,*

whatever it is and wherever it takes you? Share the reasons for your response.

- ☐ I am extremely unwilling.
- ☐ I am unwilling.
- ☐ I am somewhat unwilling.
- ☐ I am somewhat willing.
- ☐ I am willing.
- ☐ I am extremely willing.
- ☐ Other:

CHAPTER 3

FULLY QUALIFIED FOR YOUR RACE

1. Christine traced back two legacies in Kalli's life: the legacy of things that could have left her feeling disqualified for the divine relay, and then the legacy of those who carried the baton of faith into her life. Consider these same two legacies in your own life.

   - What, if anything, from your family or personal history could have left you feeling disqualified for the divine relay, for partnering with God to heal the world?
   - How far back can you trace the legacy of those who carried the baton of faith into your life?
   - In what ways have or might both legacies make you uniquely qualified not only to run the race marked out for you but also to extend batons of faith to others?

2. The story of Jesus feeding the five thousand beautifully illustrates the divine multiplication factor—how our "not enough" becomes "more than enough" when we offer it freely to God. Read the story aloud from John 6:1–12.

   - Jesus makes sure that the disciples recognize the limitations they are facing. What realities (internal or external) are you facing in this season of life that bring you face-to-face with your limitations? In other words, what is your equivalent of the five thousand hungry people? Of the young boy's meager lunch?

- When the young boy gave his not enough to Jesus, the first thing Jesus did was to bless it by giving thanks for it. What, if anything, shifts in your perspective when you consider your not enough as a gift—an asset rather than a deficit, something Jesus would celebrate and be grateful for if you willingly gave it to him?

- The miracle of more than enough happened when Jesus broke the bread and the fish. "*The miracle is in the breaking*," Christine writes. "It is in the breaking that God multiplies not enough into more than enough." What comes to mind when you consider this truth in connection with your own not enough? What is the miracle you hope for?

3. God doesn't ask you to give him something extraordinary. God is waiting for you, hoping you'll simply give him what you have, no matter how ordinary or insignificant it seems. The apostle Peter writes:

Each of you should use whatever gift you have received to serve others, as faithful stewards of God's grace in its various forms. If anyone speaks, they should do so as one who speaks the very words of God. If anyone serves, they should do so with the strength God provides, so that in all things God may be praised through Jesus Christ. To him be the glory and the power for ever and ever. Amen.

1 PETER 4:10–11, EMPHASIS ADDED

Read this passage again from *The Message*:

Be generous with the different things God gave you, passing them around so all get in on it: if words, let it be God's words;

if help, let it be God's hearty help. That way, God's bright presence will be evident in everything through Jesus, and *he'll* get all the credit as the One mighty in everything—encores to the end of time. Oh, yes!

1 PETER 4:10–11 MSG

- If you think of your not enough as a gift, what might it mean to steward it—to treat it as a resource you are responsible for using well? Even more, what might it look like to be *generous* with it?
- Peter says nothing about how big or extraordinary our acts of service should be. Instead, he emphasizes *the way* in which we are to serve, fully reliant on God. In what ways, if any, do you feel reluctant to be fully reliant on God with your not enough?
- What strength or hearty help do you need from God to become more fully reliant on him?

CHAPTER 4

EMBRACE YOUR PLACE

1. Christine defines what it means to "embrace your place" this way: "[It] means wherever you are in life, no matter what season you are in or what circumstances you face, you see yourself as an important member of God's divine relay, and you accept and do God's will today in light of his plan for all eternity."

   • You may be familiar with the phrase "know your place," which usually means to accept the fact that you are less important than others in a group. How would you describe the difference between embracing your place as Christine defines it, and knowing your place? Try to identify examples of both as part of your discussion.

   • When it comes to running the race marked out for you, what are the potential consequences of confusing these two dynamics—of defaulting to a know-your-place mindset rather than an embrace-your-place mindset?

2. Christine describes a lesson she learned in a "covered-in-vomit moment":

   The Lord has taught me that when we run the race he has marked out for us, he chooses which batons he passes us. Every leg of the race is preparation for the legs to come. . . . That day with Jeremy, I was promoted from coordinating staff to wiping vomit, and in accepting that promotion, I'd moved closer to the heart of God. . . . In order to thrive in the exchange zone, we must learn to *embrace our place.*

- It's part of human nature to rank the importance or status of things, whether it's material possessions, clothing, or careers. But there are consequences when we do this with God. How would you describe the potential consequences of ranking the importance or status of the work God calls us to do?
- Christine describes her covered-in-vomit moment as a "promotion," because it prepared her for the next legs in her race and because it moved her closer to the heart of God. What "promotions" has God offered you recently or in the past? Did you accept or decline the opportunity to embrace your place? What happened as a result?

3. Many Christians struggle to embrace their place because they feel confused, frustrated, or discouraged when the reality of serving God falls short of their expectations. Which of the following causes comes closest to describing any challenges you may have in this regard? Share the reasons for your response.

   ☐ **Obscurity and anonymity.** I feel invisible, unacknowledged, unrecognized.
   ☐ **Circumstances and trials.** I feel thwarted in what I believe I've been called to do.
   ☐ **Promotion and timing.** I feel discouraged that I'm not moving ahead as quickly as I think I should.
   ☐ **Other:**

4. Christine uses the story of David to demonstrate that we can have confidence in God's design for us—that our here and now

is God's preparation for our future, even when we can't see it or don't understand it.

- Overall, how would you describe your level of confidence in God's design and placement for your here and now? Are you the most confident you've ever been, the least confident, somewhere in between? Share the reasons for your response.

- If your here and now is God's way of preparing you for the future, how would you characterize your "training program," the means by which he is preparing you? Use one of the metaphors below or your own metaphor to describe your response.

☐ **Boot camp.** I am in an intense and rigorous program that is pushing me to my limits in every way.

☐ **Internship.** I am getting hands-on experience in an area I want to learn more about.

☐ **Physical therapy.** I am working to relieve pain or regain function in areas damaged by disease or injury.

☐ **Research.** I am in a systematic study to establish facts and reach new conclusions.

☐ **Gym workout.** I am exerting myself in intentional ways to gain health and strength.

☐ **Stress management.** I am learning ways to keep my equilibrium even in the midst of overwhelming circumstances.

☐ **Other:**

5. Like David, "We must remain faithful, committed, and loyal, even when we cannot fathom how good can come out of bad. . . . *God requires our obedience before our understanding.*" Even when we don't know what God plans to do *through* us, we do know what he plans to do *in* us—to make us more like

Jesus. "Given these truths," Christine writes, "go with what you *do* know rather than fret over what you *don't* know." Use one or more of the following prompts to identify and discuss ways you can move ahead with what you do know.

In the next twenty-four hours, I can . . .

Love God by . . .
Obey God by . . .
Trust God by . . .
Serve God by . . .
Do the next right thing by . . .

CHAPTER 5

NEVER STAND STILL IN THE EXCHANGE ZONE

1. Kristen's story is a beautiful example of what it looks like to never stand still in the exchange zone—and of why it's so important to keep running even when we hit challenges or unfamiliar territory.

   - Who has been a "Kristen" in your own life—someone who doesn't let circumstances or limitations keep them from running the race set out for them? What three to five words or phrases would you use to describe that person? What nugget of wisdom have you learned from their example?

   - The principle of never standing still in the exchange zone is so important that Christine says she now hands batons *only* to those who are already running. Briefly recall a recent baton—an invitation to allow God to work in you or through you in the world. In what ways were you already running when this baton was offered to you?

2. A veil is something that covers, protects, conceals, or separates. Two veils were lifted from Kristen's eyes: a veil that covered the shocking reality of modern-day human trafficking, and a veil that kept her from seeing the sheer magnitude of the divine relay. One veil kept her from seeing the pain of the world; the other kept her from seeing the power and goodness of God.

- If you had to define what it means to have a veil lifted, what would you say? How would you complete the sentence, *You know a veil has been lifted from your eyes when . . .*
- What veils have kept you from seeing the power and goodness of God? What veils have kept you from seeing the pain of the world? What lifted the veils?
- In Kristen's life and in your own, how would you describe the relationship between seeing the pain of the world and seeing the power and goodness of God? When the veil is lifted on one, how does it impact your ability to see the other and your ability or desire to run the race marked out for you?

3. "The Christian life is always on-the-job training," Christine writes. "God is always at work leading you, training you, and shaping your heart and passions. Just as you cannot steer a ship that isn't moving, batons cannot pass between those who are not running. God gladly steers a moving ship."

- Listed below are five nautical terms that describe changes in the movement status of a ship or vessel.[*] If you were to characterize the status of your own "ship," which term would you use? Share the reasons for your response.

  ☐ **Stopped.** A previously moving vessel moves at a speed less than 0.5 knots.[†]

  ☐ **Underway.** A previously stopped vessel moves at a speed over 3.5 knots.

  ☐ **Changed course.** A vessel changes course by certain degrees within ten minutes.

---

[*] "Vessel Movement Status Changes," marinetraffic.com, accessed 2 November 2017.

[†] A knot is a unit of speed equal to one nautical mile per hour, approximately 1.15 miles per hour.

☐ **Speed over maximum.** A vessel's speed exceeds a defined maximum limit.

☐ **Speed below minimum.** A vessel's speed drops below a defined minimum limit.

☐ **Other:**

- In what ways does the idea that God gladly steers a moving ship encourage you? In what ways does it challenge you?

4. In his letter to the church at Ephesus, the apostle Paul writes:

For we are God's handiwork, created in Christ Jesus to do good works, which God prepared in advance for us to do.

EPHESIANS 2:10

There is particular richness in two of the Greek words in this verse. The word translated "handiwork" is *poiēma* (poy-ay-mah), which literally means "poem" and suggests a "work of art." The word translated "created" is kitzō (ktid-zo). It is a verb "used only of God and denotes the creative energy he alone can exert."‡

- What do both words suggest about your identity, about who you are (and are not) in Christ Jesus?
- What do both words suggest about God's identity, about who he is (and is not)?
- If you are a work of art that God alone could create, what might that suggest about the on-the-job training potential in your current "place" (your circumstances, challenges, opportunities)? What might it suggest about God's plans for you?

---

‡ "Ephesians," A. Skevington Wood, *The Expositor's Bible Commentary*, Frank E. Gæbelein, gen. ed., vol. 11 (Grand Rapids: Zondervan, 1978), 36.

CHAPTER 6

THE MYSTERY REVEALED

1. Christine describes how, as a new believer, she experienced a spiritual reality the apostle Paul describes as "the glorious riches of this mystery, which is Christ in you" (Colossians 1:27). As a result, when the assistant youth pastor handed her a baton, Christine said yes even though it frightened her. "The old Christine would have quit before she started out of the fear of failure and not being good enough," she writes. "But the new Christine was willing, in spite of her fear, to step out in faith." Christine's experience of Christ *in* her changed her in ways she didn't always understand but could nevertheless notice.

   - Briefly recall your experiences of growth and change as a new believer. Use the following prompt to describe the ways you began to notice Christ at work in you:
   The old me would have . . . but the new me . . .
   - In what ways have you begun to notice Christ at work in you recently—in the last year, the last month, or even the last twenty-four hours? What old-me/new-me statements would you make now?

2. Discovering the power of Christ in her taught Christine three key lessons: *Rely on God's power, not your own; rely on God's resources, not your own; rely on God's ways, and not your own.*

Choose one of the following three lessons to focus on and read aloud the associated verses.

> **God's power:** Isaiah 40:28–29; Psalm 147:5; Matthew 19:26; 2 Corinthians 12:9; Ephesians 3:20–21; 2 Timothy 1:7; 2 Peter 1:3
>
> **God's resources:** Psalm 50:9–12; 84:11; Matthew 7:7–11; Luke 12:27–31; Romans 8:32; 2 Peter 1:3–4
>
> **God's ways:** Numbers 23:19; Deuteronomy 10:17; 1 Samuel 16:7; Psalm 18:30; Proverbs 3:5; Isaiah 48:17; 55:8–9

- What words or phrases stood out to you? Why?
- Contrast the truths you read about God's power/resources/ways with your own power/resources/ways. What are the key indicators that you are relying on yourself rather than God?

3. Turn to pages 82–83 and read aloud the five bulleted paragraphs that contrast what running the divine relay *is* with what it is *not*.

   - Which, if any, of the *is not* statements describe an issue you have struggled with in the past or recently? Share any examples that come to mind.
   - Which, if any, of the *is* statements intrigue you or excite you? Why?

4. It is *Christ in us* that makes us unstoppable. Christ in us both transforms us to be like him, and transforms the world through us. "Every baton displays his love and power to the world," Christine writes. "As we carry it, it changes us. . . . As long as we run, Christ in us is at work. And he never stops working in us."

   - In this season of life, which desire are you most aware of—the desire for Christ to *transform you*, or the desire for

Christ to *use you* to transform the world? Share the reasons for your response.

- How do you imagine your life might be different if you were to take this desire seriously? What difference might it make in the next twenty-four hours? The next thirty days? The next year?

CHAPTER 7

THROW IT OFF

1. After escaping a lifetime of abuse and surrendering her life to Christ, Favour realized she had to shed the hindrances—anger, bitterness, emotional scars—that kept her entangled in her old life. Otherwise, everything she'd endured had the potential to become a weapon the enemy could use against her, deepening and sustaining the harm she'd already suffered.

   - Based on your own experience and what you've witnessed in the lives of others, how would you describe what it looks like when wounds and unresolved issues become weapons the enemy uses against us?
   - The term "secondary gains" is used to describe the indirect benefits or advantages a person might get from *not* addressing an issue or a problem. For example, a woman who is afraid of feeling vulnerable or weak might hold onto anger rather than let it go because anger helps her to feel powerful and in control. Her feelings of power and control are secondary gains. In what ways might secondary gains motivate us to hold onto hindrances rather than shed them? What "benefits" might we lose by letting them go?

2. The author of the book of Hebrews writes:

Let us throw off everything that hinders and the sin that so easily entangles. And let us run with perseverance the race marked out for us.

HEBREWS 12:1

Christine identified many hindrances that might weigh us down and sins that might trip us up, several of which came from her own life. Briefly review the list below, placing a check mark next to any you may be experiencing in this season of life.

☐ Unforgiveness	☐ Selfishness
☐ Bitterness	☐ Pride
☐ Shame	☐ Unresolved anger
☐ Rejection	☐ Lack of confidence
☐ Offense	☐ Spirit of defeat
☐ Lust	☐ Lack of financial
☐ Greed	discipline
☐ Envy	☐ Regret
☐ Deceit	☐ Insecurity
☐ Insecurity	☐ Excess
☐ Fear	☐ Critical spirit
☐ Doubt	☐ Destructive
☐ Indifference	relationships
☐ Apathy	☐ Self-defeating habits
☐ False belief systems	☐ Self-indulgence
☐ Greed	☐ Past mistakes
☐ Resentment	☐ Other:

- Before discussing any of the items specifically, describe what it was like to review the list as a whole. What thoughts or emotions were you aware of as you read all of these hindrances and sins?

- To the degree you feel comfortable, talk about one or more of the items you checked. In what ways is it hindering you, entangling you, making life difficult for you?
- If you could truly throw off the hindrances and sins you identified, how do you imagine your life would be different? What would change—in your thoughts, emotions, relationships, behaviors?

3. Author and pastor Dallas Willard describes the approach we are to take in throwing off what hinders and entangles. He writes:

> To run the race well, [we must] ... take the particular things that slow us down and the sins that entangle us, and put them aside in a sensible, methodical way. We remove their roots from our minds, feelings, and so forth. We are neither hysterical nor hopeless about them. We find out what needs to be done and how to do it, and then we act. We know God will help us with every problem as we take appropriate steps. ... We don't try to accomplish everything at once, and we don't force things. If we don't immediately succeed in removing a weight or a sin, we just keep running—steadily, patiently— while we find out how it can be removed in God's way.*

- How would you describe what it means to be "hysterical" about what we are trying to throw off? To be "hopeless"? Why might we default to one of these extremes rather than choose a "sensible, methodical way"?
- What experiences, if any, have you had in trying to "accomplish everything at once" or "force things"? How would you

---

* Dallas Willard, *Renovation of the Heart: Putting on the Character of Christ* (Colorado Springs: NavPress, 2002), 253–254.

contrast these experiences with allowing hindrances and sins to be "removed in God's way"?

4. "Endings," Christine writes, "are the perfect place for a new start." What is the ending you sense God may be inviting you to make when it comes to whatever hinders or entangles in your life? What is the new start you hope for?

CHAPTER 8

MASTER THE HANDOFF

1. "Releasing the batons entrusted to your care," Christine writes, "often requires a willingness to say good-bye, to let go, to move from the known to the unknown." Generally speaking, how do you tend to respond when facing a good-bye, a change from the known to the unknown? Share the reasons for your response.

   I tend to respond with . . .

   ☐ Fear/anxiety
   ☐ Control/resistance
   ☐ Avoidance/denial
   ☐ Openness/curiosity
   ☐ Anticipation/eagerness
   ☐ Excitement/delight
   ☐ Other:

   To one degree or another, all of these responses are also evident in Annie's story. In what way does her story both challenge you and encourage you?

2. We may sometimes wonder about the details of what it is God wants us to do, but we don't have to guess about what matters most to him. When asked about the greatest commandment, Jesus gave this answer:

"Love the Lord your God with all your heart and with all your soul and with all your mind." This is the first and greatest commandment. And the second is like it: "Love your neighbor as yourself."

MATTHEW 22:37–39

Here is how one scholar elaborates on what love means in connection with both God and neighbor:

In neither case is love construed as an emotion. Love for one's neighbor means acting toward others with their good, their well-being, their fulfillment, as the primary motivation and goal of our deeds. . . . Love of God . . .is to be understood as a matter of reverence, commitment, and obedience.*

- In what ways does knowing that God's priority is love simplify or clarify your understanding of what God asks of you?
- In practical terms, how would you describe what it means to love even when you don't feel the emotion of love? What does that kind of love require of you? Share any examples of ways you or someone you know has done this.

3. Christine describes five principles for a seamless handoff, each of which includes a good-bye and a hello:
   Good-bye to bottleneck and hello to multiplication
   Good-bye to ownership and hello to stewardship
   Good-bye to control and hello to change
   Good-bye to insecurity and hello to humility
   Good-bye to the past and hello to the future

---

* Donald A. Hagner, *Matthew 14–28*, Word Biblical Commentary, Vol. 33B, Bruce M. Metzger, David A. Hubbard, and Glenn W. Barker, gen. eds. (Grand Rapids: Zondervan, 1995), 648.

- Which one or two good-byes would you say tend to be the most difficult for you? Why?
- Which one or two hellos have you learned to do well or found most rewarding? What insights or wisdom did you gain in the good-bye/hello process?

4. "You can hand off batons of faith in every relationship you encounter in your daily interactions," Christine writes. "In fact, the single most important place to run is into the lives of the people God has placed in your circle—your children, your spouse, your brother, your sister, your coworkers, your friends, and your neighbors."

- Briefly recall the interactions you had over the last twenty-four hours—morning, afternoon, and evening. Choose one of those interactions to focus on. In what small or large ways did you love this person? In other words, how did your words, demeanor, and actions affirm "their good, their well-being, their fulfillment"?
- Now look ahead to the interactions you anticipate having in the next twenty-four hours—morning, afternoon, and evening. Choose one of those interactions to focus on. How might you be intentional about using your words, demeanor, and actions to love this person?

CHAPTER 9

FUELED BY PASSION

1. Christine uses the story of how Nick pursued her to illustrate what passion looks like. "When you are passionate about someone or something," she writes, "you do not take no for an answer. You are unstoppable in your determination to find a way. You get creative.... Passion will enable you to do what you would never do if you didn't have it."

    • What stories from your own life would you use to illustrate what passion looks like? In what ways were you unstoppable in your pursuit of that something or someone?

    • What or whom is the focus of your passion lately? How have you been creative or determined in your pursuit? What does this passion enable you to do that you would never do if you didn't have it?

2. Christine defines passion for the purposes of God as "the inner spark provided by God's Holy Spirit that ignites you to your God-given purpose." Without a passion for God and his purpose for our lives, the race becomes a "have to" instead of a "want to." How would you assess your level of passion for God right now? Circle the number on the continuum (top of the next page) that best describes your response.

1	2	3	4	5	6	7	8	9	10

I have little to no passion   I am full of passion
for God. My race   for God. My race
feels like a "have to."   feels like a "want to."

- Christine says that today she is more passionate than ever to do the Lord's work. Would you say that the number you circled on the continuum represents the highest your passion for God has ever been, the lowest, or somewhere in between? Share the reasons for your response.
- When your passion for God is at its highest, what does it fuel you to do? How does it make you unstoppable, determined, creative, persevering? Share any stories or examples you can think of.

3. "Passion is not a feeling," Christine writes. "It's a decision, or a series of decisions, that fuels an ongoing love affair." She identifies five truths we can rely on to help us fuel our passion for God. Go around the group and read aloud the five statements below. As they are read, place a check mark next to the one or two statements you find especially meaningful.

    ☐ God purchased eternal life for you with the blood of his only Son, so keep your love alive by running your race out of joy, not obligation.

    ☐ God loved you before you loved him, so keep your love alive by telling him you love him . . . every single day.

    ☐ God speaks his love into your life, so read his love letter to you—the Bible—daily.

    ☐ God rejoices over you with singing, so keep your love alive by giving him your thanks and praise.

    ☐ God heals your pain and brings healing into your life, so display your love to him by bringing healing to others.

- Which statements did you check? How do these truths help to fuel your passion for God?
- How do you respond to the idea that passion is not a feeling but a series of decisions? In what ways, if any, do you recognize this truth in connection with the things or people about which you are passionate?
- Take a moment now to follow through on the second truth by telling God you love him. First, share with the group a recent experience in which God conveyed his love and care for you. It might have been something very small or something bigger, but in that moment you received it as evidence of God's love for you.
- Once everyone has shared, close your time together by going around the group again, this time expressing your love directly to God in prayer. Keep your prayers simple and brief, just two or three sentences. Thank God for the experience of his love you just described, and then express your love for him.

CHAPTER 10

THE MAKING OF A CHAMPION

1. "God's divine relay threatens the enemy's territory," Christine writes, "and he will not go down without a fight." Author C. S. Lewis echoes this theme when he writes:

Enemy-occupied territory—that is what this world is. Christianity is the story of how the rightful king has landed, you might say landed in disguise, and is calling us all to take part in a great campaign of sabotage.*

Sabotage is a deliberate action aimed at weakening an opponent through subversion, obstruction, disruption, or destruction. A *campaign* is a systematic course of aggressive activities designed to destroy, damage, or obstruct something to gain advantage.
   - Using the above definitions of *sabotage* and *campaign* as a reference, how would you describe what it means to engage in a spiritual campaign of sabotage?
   - Chapter 8 explored how love is God's number one priority. How might love be an act of "sabotage"?

---

* C. S. Lewis, *Mere Christianity* (San Francisco: HarperOne, 1952, 1980), 46.

2. In any war, opposing sides engage in both offensive and defensive strategies. An *offensive* strategy seeks to gain new territory, damage enemy assets, or achieve a larger strategic objective. A *defensive* strategy seeks to protect one's own territory and assets from loss or harm. Consider the implications this might have for spiritual battle.

   - What offensive and defensive strategies does the enemy engage in?
   - What offensive and defensive strategies does the "rightful king" engage in?
   - How do these strategies of the enemy and of the rightful king tend to play out in human lives? Consider examples from the story Christine tells about Phil at the beginning of the chapter, as well as examples from your own life or the lives of those you know.
   - In what ways, if any, do the metaphor and strategies of war shift your perspective on your own challenges and struggles?

3. "The enemy is already defeated," Christine writes. "And what's more, God uses the enemy's tactics against him. What the enemy intends for evil, God uses for good. . . . God uses every single trial to our benefit."

   Many verses in the Bible affirm that God is not the author of evil (Deuteronomy 32:4; 1 Corinthians 14:33; James 1:13; 1 John 1:5). He does not *cause* our suffering, but he does *redeem* it. To redeem is to save, buy back, or make an exchange. God never wastes our trials.

   - Take a moment to think back on trials from your past. In what ways, if any, would you say God has used these hardships for your benefit? What good things are true of who you are or of your life now that might not otherwise be true?

- If you could go back in time and speak a word of encouragement, comfort, or wisdom to your past self in the midst of those trials, what might you say?
- In what ways, if any, do the words you might say to your past self provide encouragement, comfort, or wisdom for the trials you face now?

4. Trials have the potential to be the ultimate strength-training exercise, to help us become God's champions. In fact, James actually encourages us to "consider it pure joy . . . whenever you face trials of many kinds" (James 1:2). *The Message* puts it this way:

Consider it a sheer gift, friends, when tests and challenges come at you from all sides. You know that under pressure, your faith-life is forced into the open and shows its true colors. So don't try to get out of anything prematurely. Let it do its work so you become mature and well-developed, not deficient in any way.

JAMES 1:2–4 MSG

- When recently was your faith-life "forced into the open"? What "true colors" did you discover about yourself and about your faith that you might not otherwise have known?
- What do you think it means to let tests and challenges do their work? In other words, how can we allow them to bring out the best rather than the worst in us, to strengthen us rather than weaken us? As part of your discussion, consider any insights from the stories Christine told about Phil or the apostle Peter, and any from your own life as well.

CHAPTER 11

OUTRUNNING THE PASSION SLAYERS

1. Christine uses the illustration of a tiny black dot on a large white space to illustrate the importance of what we choose to focus on. She writes:

   The black dots of our lives—the trials, challenges, disappointments, obstacles, and hurdles we face as we run—will naturally draw and consume our attention . . . but in the divine relay, we are to fix our eyes on Jesus. He is the "white space" of God's power at work in the universe, and the trials we face are but a tiny speck, a black dot, in comparison.

   - When we *focus* on something, we give most of our attention to it. We concentrate on it, discuss it, or work on it to the exclusion of other things. Briefly reflect on any "black dots" in your life right now and the degree to which they occupy your focus. Consider one or more of the following questions: How often do you find your thoughts concentrating on these dots? To what degree do these dots show up in your conversations? How much time do you devote to working on them?

   Seventeenth-century author and pastor Thomas Watson writes:

The first fruit of love is the musing of the mind upon God.... God is the treasure, and where the treasure is, there is the heart. By this we may test our love to God. What are our thoughts most upon?[*]

- We tend to think of our thought life as a solo operation, but part of what Watson's statement suggests is that our thought life is actually relational—what we focus on has the potential to strengthen our love for God or to weaken it. How do you respond to this idea, and to Watson's statement?
- Focus requires a choice. "Whatever I chose to focus on had my attention," Christine writes. "There is *always* much more white space than there is space covered by little black dots—we simply need to recognize and focus on it." Take a few moments to fix your eyes on Jesus by recognizing and focusing on the "white space" surrounding your black dots. In what ways do you recognize God's power at work—on your behalf, in your circumstances, in you, through you, in the world around you? What evidence do you have that God is active in your life, that he is good and worthy of your trust?

2. "Passion-slayers" are common ways the enemy works to draw our focus to the black dots of our lives and to sow discontentment. Briefly review the list of eight common passion slayers, focusing for now only on the words in bold. Place a check mark next to one or two that have diminished your passion recently.

☐ **Negative circumstances.** What good might God be doing—in me and through me—that I can't yet see?
☐ **Fear.** How might God use this to strengthen my trust?

---

[*] Thomas Watson, *All Things for Good* (1663: reprint, Carlisle, PA: The Banner of Truth Trust, 1986), 74.

- ☐ **Failure.** How can I allow God to use this to build my character?
- ☐ **Unmet expectations.** How might God use this to expand my reach?
- ☐ **Relational strife.** How might God be inviting me to love like Jesus?
- ☐ **Weariness.** What might I need to relinquish so I can rest in God and trust his timing?
- ☐ **Opposition.** How might God be using this to achieve his goals—in my life and in the world?
- ☐ **Hopelessness.** How might I reach toward hope, believing that God has a way even when I see no way?
- ☐ **Other:**

- Share the passion-slayers you checked. Briefly explain how they have diminished your passion or made it difficult for you to focus on the "white space" of God's power at work in your life.
- Once again, practice focusing on the white space by responding to the questions listed with the passion-slayers you checked.

3. We outrun passion-slayers by learning to be content in the midst of our trials.

I have learned to be content whatever the circumstances. I know what it is to be in need, and I know what it is to have plenty. I have learned the secret of being content in any and every situation, whether well fed or hungry, whether living in plenty or in want.

PHILIPPIANS 4:11–12

When Paul twice says he has "learned," the Greek word he uses is *manthanō* (man-than-o). It means to acquire a habit, or to learn by practice or experience. In other words, learning to be content was not something Paul read somewhere and then mentally filed away for future reference. He learned how to be content by *practicing*.

- Practice requires doing something regularly in order to be able to do it better. Briefly identify and describe one thing in your life you practice already. What are your habits or disciplines around that practice? What pro tips might your current practice provide about what it means to learn and practice contentment in your black-dot circumstances?

- Acquiring a habit of contentment enables us to see potential passion-slayers as "nothing more than God's opportunity to defeat the enemy and complete his good work." What is the good work you hope God might do in you and through you as you navigate your black dots?

CHAPTER 12

THE WINNER'S CIRCLE

1. Jesus' legacy of self-sacrifice is the most remarkable and startling legacy in the history of our planet. Here is how the apostle Paul describes it:

> Have the same mindset as Christ Jesus: Who, being in very nature God, did not consider equality with God something to be used to his own advantage; rather, he made himself nothing by taking the very nature of a servant, being made in human likeness. And being found in appearance as a man, he humbled himself by becoming obedient to death—even death on a cross!
>
> PHILIPPIANS 2:5–8

Read the passage once more, this time from *The Message*:

> Think of yourselves the way Christ Jesus thought of himself. He had equal status with God but didn't think so much of himself that he had to cling to the advantages of that status no matter what. Not at all. When the time came, he set aside the privileges of deity and took on the status of a slave, became *human*! Having become human, he stayed human. It was an incredibly humbling process. He didn't claim special privileges. Instead, he lived a selfless, obedient life and then died a selfless, obedient death—and the worst kind of death at that—a crucifixion.
>
> PHILIPPIANS 2:5–8 MSG

- A legacy is something someone has achieved or given that continues to exist after they are gone. Put simply, a legacy is a gift that keeps on giving. How, specifically, is Jesus' life of self-sacrifice a "legacy"? What gifts have you received because of this legacy? What gifts have you given because of this legacy?

- The question is not *if* we will leave a legacy, but rather *what* our legacy will be. Consider the legacy you hope to leave, not by focusing on your lifetime overall but by focusing on the immediate future. What legacy would you like to leave in the day ahead? In what ways might you give lasting gifts by living a selfless, obedient life for twenty-four hours?

- Now play the movie forward. How might your twenty-four-hour legacy accumulate when lived out over the course of a week, a month, a year? In what ways, if any, does thinking about your twenty-four-hour legacy help you to imagine the kind of lifetime legacy you hope to leave behind—for your loved ones as well as for the kingdom?

2. Christine uses the story of Jesus' surrender to God in Gethsemane to describe the "Winner's Cup" we accept when we choose to follow Christ:

And he was withdrawn from them about a stone's throw, and he knelt down and prayed, saying, "Father, if it is Your will, take this cup away from Me; nevertheless not My will, but Yours, be done."

LUKE 22:41–42 NKJV

"The Winner's Cup is SACRIFICIAL LOVE," Christine writes. "In one powerful word—*nevertheless*—he surrendered all to the will of his Father. . . . [We] accept this Winner's Cup [when] we lay down *our* lives and pour out *ourselves* in living sacrifice to God."

- Jesus doesn't deny his will, denigrate it, or try to force himself to want it less. He can both acknowledge his will and surrender it because there is something he wants *more*—the will of the Father. How does it influence your understanding of surrender to think of it as wanting more rather than wanting less?
- To better understand the power of sacrificial love, consider your experiences on the receiving end of such love. Who made a sacrificial choice—small or large—to love you in some way? What did they sacrifice? How did their actions, words, and demeanor convey love? How did this sacrificial love impact you?
- Based on the experience you just described, complete the following sentence: *I know I am making a choice to love sacrificially when . . .*

3. Christine describes how she and the people she writes about—Kalli, Kristen, Favour, Annie, Phil—are continuing to live out their "nevertheless" (pages 170–171). Drawing on their examples, how would you describe your nevertheless—the ways in which you are choosing to surrender yourself to God's will in this season of life?

4. "There is no retirement from the race this side of heaven," Christine writes. "As long as you have breath in your body, you can breathe God's love into this world." What does breathing God's love into this world require of you today?

Unashamed

Drop the Baggage, Pick up Your Freedom, Fulfill Your Destiny

Christine Caine

Shame can take on many forms. It hides in the shadows of the most successful, confident and high-achieving woman who struggles with balancing her work and children, as well as in the heart of the broken, abused and downtrodden woman who has been told that she will never amount to anything. Shame hides in plain sight and can hold us back in ways we do not realize. But Christine Caine wants readers to know something: we can all be free.

"I know. I've been there," writes Christine. "I was schooled in shame. It has been my constant companion from my very earliest memories. I see shame everywhere I look in the world, including in the church. It creeps from heart to heart, growing in shadowy places, feeding on itself so that those struggling with it are too shamed to seek help from shame itself."

In *Unashamed*, Christine reveals the often-hidden consequences of shame—in her own life and the lives of so many Christian women—and invites you to join her in moving from a shame-filled to a shame-free life.

In her passionate and candid style, Christine leads you into God's Word where you will see for yourself how to believe that God is bigger than your mistakes, your inadequacies, your past, and your limitations. He is more powerful than anything you've done and stronger than anything ever done to you. You can deal with your yesterday today, so that you can move on to what God has in store for you tomorrow—a powerful purpose and destiny he wants you to fulfill.

Join the journey. Lay ahold of the power of Jesus Christ today and step into the future—his future for you—a beautiful, full, life-giving future, where you can even become a shame-lifter to others. Live unashamed!

Unashamed Video Curriculum
Drop the Baggage, Pick up Your Freedom, Fulfill Your Destiny

Christine Caine

In this five-session video Bible study, author and teacher Christine Caine weaves examples from her life with those of biblical characters who failed but overcame their shame to show how God heals us and redeems us. In her passionate style, she explains that if we want to change our futures, we have to believe God is bigger than our mistakes, our inadequacies, our pasts, and our limitations. We have to believe God created us for a unique purpose, has a specific plan for us, and has a powerful destiny he wants us to fulfill.
Session titles include:

- Session 1: Run, Don't Hide (Run to Jesus, Don't Hide from Jesus)
- Session 2: Today Is the Day (Shame Off You Today)
- Session 3: Possess Your Inheritance (You Must Go In and Take It)
- Session 4: God Never Wastes a Hurt (Our Scars Can Become a Sign of Victory, Not Shame)
- Session 5: Highly Unlikely (God Uses Ordinary People to Achieve Extraordinary Results)

The companion study guide (DVD sold separately) will lead you and your group deeper into the video content with guided session-by-session discussion questions, personal reflection questions, and between-sessions studies to enhance the group experience.

Undaunted

Daring to do what God calls you to do

Christine Caine

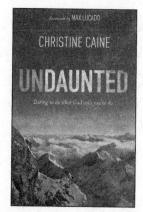

Christine Caine is no superhero. She's just like you. And she is changing the world.

Using her own dramatic life story, Christine shows how God rescued her from a life in which she was unnamed, unwanted, and unqualified. She overcame abuse, abandonment, fears, and other challenges to go on a mission of adventure, fueled by faith and filled with love and courage.

Christine offers life-transforming insights about not only how to overcome the trials, wrong turns, and often painful circumstances we all experience, but also how to grow from those experiences and be equipped and empowered to help others.

Her personal stories will inspire you to hear your own name called—just as Christine heard hers—to go into a dark and troubled world. Each of us possesses all it takes to bring hope, create change, and live completely for Christ.

Unshakeable

365 Devotions for Finding Unwavering Strength in God's Word

Christine Caine

God is bigger than your current story. Bigger than fear or shame or that voice in your head that whispers that you are not enough, too broken, or too flawed. Join him in a closer relationship—one rooted in truth and *Unshakeable*. In this yearlong daily devotional, bestselling author, speaker and activist Christine Caine encourages you to find confidence to live as the person God created you to be.

Everything in our world that can be shaken will be shaken. And yet, the Bible assures us it doesn't matter what happens politically, morally, socially, or economically in the world around us if we have Christ in us—if we have the kingdom of God within us—because his kingdom is *Unshakeable*.

Through inspiring personal stories and powerful Scriptures, Christine Caine will equip you to live boldly and courageously, fully trusting our faithful God. She will inspire you how to activate living your life on mission. Unstoppable. Undaunted. Unashamed. *Unshakeable*.

> *"All of creation will be shaken and removed, so that only unshakable things will remain."*—Hebrews 12:27 NLT

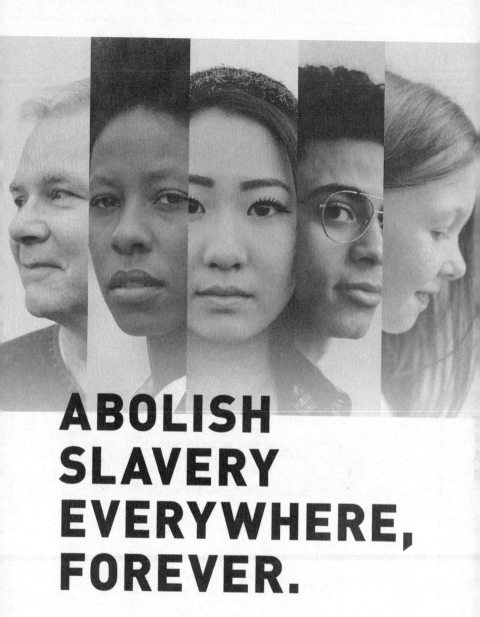

ABOLISH SLAVERY EVERYWHERE, FOREVER.

 A21.ORG  @A21campaign   @A21 @A21

Ignite your

PASSION.

Cultivate your

PURPOSE.

Realize your

POTENTIAL.

PROPEL WOMEN

For articles, videos and other free resources,
visit **www.PropelWomen.org**!

@PROPELWOMEN